THE ♥OTHER W♥MAN

Dr. Godwin Ude

THE OTHER
WOMAN

For The Woman Who Loves Her
Man Enough To Fight For His Soul

TATE PUBLISHING
AND ENTERPRISES, LLC

Published by Tate Publishing & Enterprises, LLC
127 E. Trade Center Terrace | Mustang, Oklahoma 73064 USA
1.888.361.9473 | www.tatepublishing.com

Tate Publishing is committed to excellence in the publishing industry. The company reflects the philosophy established by the founders, based on Psalm 68:11,
"The Lord gave the word and great was the company of those who published it."

Published in the United States of America

ISBN: 978-1-62295-623-4
Family & Relationships / Marriage
12.11.13

INTRODUCTION

T he solution you may be looking for on how to resolve what you consider a difficult challenge in your marriage may be in the book you are holding in your hands now. Have you wondered why couples who began their journey with a flame of passion for each other that seemed unquenchable quickly fall into relational doldrums within months after exchanging vows? Have you tried to figure out what the infamous words "irreconcilable differences" mean? Within this book, you will make amazing discoveries that will be refreshing and restoring to your marriage.

The purpose of a marital relationship is the merging of two souls into one. This union is a mystery beyond any psychoanalysis or spiritual explanations. The excitement that surrounds marriage celebrations can simply be described as exhilarating. Women look forward to their wedding day and use the greater part of their young adult lives preparing for it.

But oftentimes, the flame of marital love and oneness dwindles as fast as it was ignited. Gradually, what was made to be one begins to be torn apart by almost invisible causes too subtle to discover until they unleash their venom on a marriage.

Unfortunately, very few couples are equipped to deal with this inevitable obstacle on their way to oneness. In trying to grasp the reality of losing the initial flame of passion, couples may seek something to replace that which has been lost outside the marriage domain.

Men are by nature adventurous. This natural disposition can cause them to share the oneness designed only for their spouse with someone or *something* else. Note the emphasis on *something*. What so many fail to realize when marital problems arise is that there are several factors outside of extramarital love affairs that can shake the foundation of a marriage.

I refer to these often-overlooked factors as "other women." As a man's passion for these "other women" increases, his ability to connect with his spouse will continue to diminish, and this can lead to mounting subtle frictions in the relationship. Because these "other women" are understated in nature, they are often hidden from the professional eyes of marriage counselors— and even from the couples themselves. After attempting series of counseling sessions or marriage mentoring without success, women often conclude that their husbands are seeing other women. In some instances, this may be the case, but looking at the reality of many marriages reveals that most men are addicted to what I call the "other woman," which, more times than not, doesn't involve another woman at all.

This work is designed to uncover some of these "other women" and demonstrate how they can steal the soul of men from their beloved spouses. This has been a missing weapon in the arsenals of those trained to help marriages as counselors and mentors.

The purpose of this work is not to provide a comprehensive counseling service but to offer you practical tips on how to start working toward restoring intimacy in your marriage. I am an advocate of seeking qualified Christian counselors in matters beyond frank conversations with your spouse. It is assumed that the issues discussed here as the "other women" are obvious problems affecting marriages that need no elaborate explanations or deep theological insights to determine whether such "other woman" is a problem, sin, or simply a misdemeanor. Hence, I deliberately limited the use of scriptural quotations and other reference materials in order to facilitate the ease of reading and comprehension and also reach many who desperately need this information. The goal is to point out these problems and suggest ways of dealing with them.

It is important to bear in mind that men can allocate their passion to anything they are fascinated with, and this can mean that hobbies can take energy that should be devoted to the marriage. The primary goal of the information provided here is to bring the range of "other women" that may be affecting a relationship to light in order to begin the rebuilding process that is needed to save a sinking marriage. In this book, we will journey through some true stories with fictitious characters and discuss the various "other women" that have robbed your marriage and has laid claim to your husband. Any resemblance of persons and names mentioned in this book to real persons should be considered coincidental. Within the body of this book, we will also identify how you can be a part of the solution.

Each chapter has been designed to make reading enjoyable without losing focus. The stories are included to illustrate the issues discussed and to demonstrate real life applications along with exemplary narratives. The purpose is to present you with a handbook of helpful information that will transform your marital relationship in a way that you have only imagined.

Though this book is written with the mission to help women deal with some common male-related dysfunctions in a marriage relationship from a redemptive perspective, women are encouraged to share this book with their husbands. However, look out for the sequel titled *The Other Man*, written in the same style with the same purpose but targeted to husbands, just as this one is targeted to wives.

For men reading this book, be careful of whom and what you give your soul to outside of your marriage. For women reading this book, this will arm you to fight for the soul of the love of your life and to reclaim it from the "other women" who have taken what belongs to you.

Happy reading!

CHAPTER 1:

MEET THE "OTHER WOMAN"

DON AND YVETTE'S DISTRACTION DILEMMA

The morning dew was refreshing to Don as he grabbed his camera bag and keys to his sleek, black sports car. He quickly glanced around the living room to make sure he hadn't forgotten anything and stepped out of the door. Don took a deep breath in and quickly trotted off to his car. As he loaded up the car, he saw a text come across his phone.

"Goodbye, I guess," it read from his wife, Yvette.

Don shrugged his shoulders and continued loading his car. He slid into the new leather seats and started the engine. He sighed deeply, placed the car into gear, and sped off down the road toward the highway. He made a quick pit stop to grab an energy bar and fill up the gas tank. Don had a three-hour drive ahead of him.

As he drove along the almost empty highway, it was early and a Saturday morning, so no one was out yet. Don couldn't stop thinking about the constant nagging he had been getting from Yvette. She was never happy. He would much rather feel the speed and power of his sports car or hide behind the lens of his camera than spend time with a woman whom he knew would pick him apart at every opportunity. Don's thoughts drifted from his hard-to-please wife to an old friend whose number he still had. He reached for his phone, scrolled down his contacts, and began to dial.

"Hello, Lori," Don said.

"Hey, mister!" Lori chimed back. "What's going on?"

"I'm off to the car show and then headed back through the mountains to grab some awesome pictures of the scenery. I'm on the highway now. What are your plans for today?" Don bubbled out with excitement.

"Oh, not much," Lori replied sleepily. "Just working and hanging with the kids today. I am glad you are so excited. Have fun and definitely send me some pictures of those awesome cars and the mountains! Call me when you get there."

"Great. Talk to you later, young lady," Don said, smiling as he hung up the phone.

Don continued driving for a couple of hours until he reached his destination. The car show was already packed, and it was only seven in the morning. Don paid his entrance fee, found his spot, and parked his car. *What a day this will be*, Don thought with a smile.

Back at home, Yvette was just beginning to wake up. It was time to take out the dog and get ready to visit her mother. Yvette was a little disturbed as she glanced down at her phone and saw that Don had still not responded to her text.

Yvette felt like lately Don was more interested in his hobbies than her. At the beginning of their relationship, she loved his passions and hobbies, but at that stage, he also seemed to hang on her every word. Since their marriage, however, he had begun to distance himself from her. He still had the passion for photography and sports cars that he did when their relationship was budding, but his passion for her seemed to have faded. Yvette knew that she could be overbearing at times, but that is how she always had been. She sometimes wondered if her headstrong personality was an issue for her husband, but she would always come to the conclusion that her strong personality was something that attracted her husband to her. She could not figure out what it was that was causing so much tension and so little intimacy. They had been in marriage counseling once, and, because they weren't consistent, there wasn't much that became of it.

Yvette slumped down onto the living room sofa, stared down at her phone that had no new text messages, and wondered if this new marriage of only four years was going to survive. Meanwhile, Don was showing his car and snapping photos of other cars he admired. Looking at the time, he realized that in just one hour he would be off to the mountains! This was the life….

Cheating on a spouse with another lover is, to most, the ultimate betrayal. In fact, it is one of the most common reasons that marriages end. What most people don't know is that the "other woman" who drives a wedge into a relationship isn't always a woman at all. Men who do not stray to another woman often find just as destructive distractions in their hobbies, career, or even platonic friendships. Though not adulterous, this distraction from intimacy is equally troubling and detrimental to a healthy relationship.

When a husband cheats with another woman, it's a straightforward situation. How you choose to resolve that betrayal is up to you, but the circumstances are pretty clear: for one reason or another, your husband may have found ways to meet his assumed or real unmet needs through intimacy with another person. But oftentimes your husband may have found an outlet other than a love affair, however, to compensate for something he feels is missing in your marriage. He is no anomaly in doing so, either. Many men turn to hobbies or become fixated with their careers to mask their marital problems. While immersing himself in something other than your shared life probably isn't something that was mentioned during your marriage vows, it is something that can cause major rifts in your relationship.

Fortunately, there are ways you can bring your husband's attention back to your relationship. The process of restoring a strained marriage begins with addressing the distraction within the marriage and bringing the focus back to the relationship. After the groundwork has been laid and the problem addressed, open communication and a willingness from both husband and wife to work with one another to mend what has been broken is vital in overcoming the obstacle that is deterring you from having the marriage that God intended you to have.

GETTING TO THE SOURCE OF THE PROBLEM

A marriage is meant to be a mutually supportive and beneficial arrangement that provides companionship, as well as celebrates and nurtures the most powerful of human emotions—love. A distracted spouse has not necessarily fallen out of love with their partner. Oftentimes, a spouse who spends his time and energy outside of his relationship is either afraid of something found in intimacy or is attempting to meet needs his partner has been unable to satisfy.

If your husband directs his attention and energy toward activities outside your marriage, he is likely avoiding some aspect of intimacy. The following are some of the reasons that men will turn from their wives to external distractions. Which are most likely true in your situation?

- Inadequate intimacy levels in marital relationship
- Unsure how to create and grow within marital intimacy
- Inability to move beyond stressors and conflict when around spouse
- Having different life goals than spouse
- Feeling pressured to be a certain person when around spouse
- Not enough pleasure in marital relationship

This list mentions just a few of the main reasons men have been known to change focus from their marriage to personal hobbies and other distractions.

TAKING THE FIRST STEPS: WHAT YOU CAN DO

As a wife, it is easier for you to notice your husband's withdrawal. This is not to say that you will be able to fix the situation on your own. However, you will need to work with your husband to create the marital environment you both need. Amos 3:3 (NIV) asks, "Do two walk together unless they have agreed to do so?" Both you and your husband will eventually need to be on the same page when it comes to improving the intimacy and communication within your relationship.

No matter how hard you work or how many sacrifices you make, some men will simply be unwilling to work through the marital problems at hand. Until you decide your spouse is completely unwilling to do his part in repairing your relationship, make sure you clearly and openly communicate your concerns with him. There are a number of ways that you can create an open dialogue with your husband that will ensure that you are clearly conveying the issues arising in your marriage. Here are some key points to keep in mind when you decide to approach your husband:

- An observant partner points out the change of focus when their partner becomes distracted by external stimuli.

- A communicative partner lets their distracted partner know the problems and the change in focus that has caused a wedge in the marriage.

- A humble and committed partner is ready to take the steps to improve their marriage so that both people in the relationship are getting their needs met.

- Marriage is a mutual commitment to striving for a happy, supportive life. Both partners must be involved for success in this arena.

Of course, this process should also always respect your own needs and concerns as well as your husband's. Giving up your own interests and goals for the sake of creating harmony in your marriage might get you some renewed attention to begin with, but ultimately the real reasons your husband turned his focus away will arise, and you will be back at square one.

DON'T FORGET ABOUT YOU

Because marriage involves mutual sacrifice and concession, keeping your own needs and goals in mind is essential to reestablishing your intimate marriage. If you make your husband happy but you are miserable, your efforts will have been for naught. Always remember that your ultimate goal is mutual happiness; that means your well-being matters, too.

It is okay if you don't know your long-term goals for yourself right now. You can find and realize those during the process of repairing your marriage. Just remember to keep your happiness and well-being in high regard to avoid trading your husband's happiness for your own and placing yourself in a one-sided relationship. Remember that the ideal outcome is for both you and your spouse to be happy, supported, ready, and willing for intimacy.

CREATING COMMUNICATION: THE KEY TO MARRIAGE SUCCESS

The tricky part of rebuilding a damaged marriage is getting your husband to talk. Men are famous for their ability to draw their emotions deep inside themselves and let them fester without ever addressing them head-on. This is not a flaw in men; it is a part of them that makes them who they are, which has both positive and negative consequences. To repair your marriage, you'll need to help your husband reach deep inside him and pull out those emotions he has been hoarding and hiding.

Your husband's unmet needs are likely ones he has never expressed to you. As a woman, you may be thinking, *But if I don't know what his needs are, how am I supposed to meet them?* Women tend to be better at communicating their needs to their spouses, but men often internalize issues that arise and attempt to handle them in their own ways. The most important tool that you can possess when helping your husband explore the feelings he's kept locked away is patience.

A qualified Christian marriage therapist, though terrifying to many men, can help your husband open up and access his emotions. Often, men are too unsure or feel too vulnerable expressing feelings to do the emotional footwork that is needed to work on a marriage without any outside help. An experienced Christian marriage counselor can help your confused husband figure out what it is that is driving him away from you and the intimacy a marital relationship requires.

Of course, getting your husband to actually go to therapy might be a challenge in and of itself. Many men view therapy as scary, pointless, or foolish. Our society has taught men that being in touch with their emotions is a trait that rests outside the realm of masculinity and is a weakness rather than an asset. This is terribly unfortunate, as open communication and a willingness to risk vulnerability is imperative to creating a healthy, supportive, and mutually satisfying relationship.

If you're having trouble convincing your husband to give therapy a try, try the following to make him more willing to take this big step to resolving your marital concerns:

- If your pastor is not equipped to handle this kind of challenge, ask him or any of your family friends, particularly those who are married, if they have therapist recommendations.

- Seek out a Christian therapist who specializes in working with men.

- Find a therapist who has experience with your unique situation.

- Find men that your husband respects who have had positive experiences with therapy.

- Be willing to talk through your husband's concerns with him.

- Share books or articles that talk about men in therapy with your husband.

- Communicate clearly and calmly you're your husband's participation in attending therapy would be a big relief for you.

Being supportive of your husband as he reaches out is paramount to him becoming more open with his emotions. Finding support in your circle of friends will also help him feel encouraged and supported.

RECOMMITTING

Deciding that this man and this relationship are something worth fighting for is imperative to succeeding in bringing your husband's focus back to your marriage. Before you can begin to truly repair the intimacy in your relationship, you must be confident that this relationship is worth your time, effort, sacrifice, and energy.

After experiencing distractions, repairing your marriage will require commitment, determination, and a lot of hard work to fully recover. You will both need to be sure you are ready to do the work to succeed. For most couples, the desire to recommit to the marriage is something that fluctuates, occasionally or regularly, depending on where they are in the recovery process. Ultimately, how quickly and clearly you both commit to the relationship will determine how quickly your marriage recovers.

THE IMPACT OF THE "OTHER WOMAN"

The "other woman" by nature is many different types of distractions that a marriage may experience. This distraction that we call the "other woman" can have many devastating effects on the marriage. This "woman" ultimately interferes with the level of intimacy, trust, and companionship that exists in a marriage.

INTIMACY

Having intimacy in a marriage is vital. Intimacy is a place inside an individual in which he or she has opened his or her heart and soul to vulnerability in order to create a new level of closeness with another person. This is a place where the deepest levels of emotions, fears, and thoughts can be shared. When the "other woman" begins to take your place in your husband's list of emotional priorities, the shift of focus leaves a void in that intimate place in your relationship. Many times, you feel the void before you notice what is taking your place. This causes natural and instinctual responses to regain your position. These responses, if not controlled, can drive your spouse farther away. You must approach this void in intimacy carefully and wisely.

TRUST

Trust in a marriage is an essential component. Trust implies that what you do or say can be taken at face value. When trust operates as it should in a marriage, the couple is not concerned with every detail of one another's daily activities. There are no nagging uncertainties or jealousy issues that must be dealt with on a day-to-day basis. When your husband begins spending more time with the "other woman," you begin to lose your confidence in his reliability, thus you lose your confidence in his devotion to your marriage; you no longer *trust* his every word. This is a detrimental loss in the relationship, as losing trust is devastating and not easy to regain.

COMPANIONSHIP

One of the main purposes for marriage is companionship.

> Two are better than one, because they have a good return for their labor: If either of them falls down, one can help the other up. But pity anyone who falls and has no one to help them up. Also, if two lie down together, they will keep warm. But how can one keep warm alone…?
>
> Ecclesiastes 4:9-12

Most of us are looking for that person who will become our lifetime companion. A companion is a friend, lover, and a partner. This multidimensional aspect of marriage can actually produce the most harmful effects on the relationship. Many times, when one aspect of marriage begins to slip, as long as you still feel that you're not alone and have a companion, you feel less isolated in the marriage even though there may be a piece of the relationship that needs work. When the "other woman" steals the companionship that you share with your husband, however, you begin to feel cut off from him. This emotional seclusion can leave feelings of betrayal and helplessness in its wake.

The tensions created by the "other woman" can truly destroy your marriage unless you become proactive in saving it. Many times, it's easy to point the finger when someone or something replaces you in your husband's life. If he searches to fulfill a level of intimacy elsewhere, then maybe some self-examination should be done as well.

NOW WHAT: THE NEXT STEPS TO A HEALTHY MARRIAGE

Now that you have established that your husband is turning his back on you by disappearing into some activity that is meeting his needs, what do you do?

First, count your blessings. You have a man by your side whom you are willing to work to keep. Love and companionship are the cream of life; always remember the good things that made you fall in love in the first place. This positive thinking will give you the energy and stamina to make it through the worst of times.

Second, pat yourself on the back. Noticing that your husband is slipping away and having the clarity of mind to seek a solution demonstrates your faith and commitment to your marriage. It is rarely as easy as happily ever after. A lasting relationship requires work, but the reward is a lifetime of growing, learning, and living beside someone you trust deeply.

Lastly, and most importantly, you will want to make some commitments to yourself in regard to your marriage and the ways that you are ready to work to make it what you long for it to be. You need to be specific in what you want to accomplish and be sure you are willing to really work toward the goals that you set.

WORKING OUT THE PROBLEM

Before you can begin a successful endeavor to change your marriage for the better, you need to have a clear idea of what it is you want from yourself, your husband, and your shared life. Many people are pulled in several directions by whatever distraction seems most appealing in the moment. To consistently make intentional decisions gives you the power of will and allows you to fully realize yourself and your dreams.

The first step to exercising your will is to decide what it is you want. Writing down your objectives will help make them more tangible and accomplishable. The following are some writing exercises that will help you name your goals:

1. Get a few pieces of paper and a pen. If you have a journal, you can use that to keep track of your goals.

2. Start writing about what is most troubling to you right now within your marriage. List all your irritants along with the things that are complicating your life and causing you to doubt your commitment.

3. Focus on specifics as much as possible. This will help you pinpoint where changes need to occur.

4. If there is a certain action that is bothering you, how does it make you feel when your husband does it? Why do you think it makes you feel that way? How do you think it makes him feel?

Follow your questions through; be your own therapist.

By following these writing prompts, you will be completing a guided brainstorm that will help you identify the very root of the problem that is causing you strife. This is a basic writing exercise that can give you insight with just about any problem in your life. In this case, you can use it to clarify what you want when you begin the conversation with your husband to repair your marriage.

BEGINNING THE CONVERSATION

Find a time when you are both well rested and in pleasant moods to begin the conversation. Knowing what it is you want, the details of the problem your husband is struggling with, and being able to articulate how it is negatively affecting your marriage will be exactly what you need to communicate the situation.

THE BLAME GAME: A ROAD TO NOWHERE

More often than not, it is not something that a woman has or has not done that causes a man to lose interest in his marriage. Because good communication is a rare skill in today's society, your husband not opening up to you about his concerns and unmet needs is also not entirely his fault, either. Sometimes these communication breakdowns just occur. In response to the confusion or frustration in the marriage, many men will find a hobby to hide inside rather than confront the problem at hand. Try not to blame yourself or your partner for this inherent part of masculinity. Like many sticky situations in marriage, a distracted spouse needs to be addressed and remedied with the involvement of both partners. Blame and fault are less important than fixing the problem and meeting the unmet needs that originally caused the conflict.

When beginning the conversation with your husband about your concerns, remember to be humble. Don't begin a discussion with your husband with a self-righteous tone. Come to him as an equal, appealing for help. You, too, most likely have played some part in the problem. Be as ready to shoulder the responsibility that is yours as you are to point out his mistakes. Approaching marital issues in this way lets your husband know that you two are a team fighting for the same side, not adversaries pitted against one another. It also demonstrates that you realize the problem is a mutual problem, not just his. If you want to be successful in solving your marital issues, do what you can to avoid putting your husband on the defense. A defensive partner is much less likely to be receptive to possible solutions.

Also, gone are the days of wives being always blamed for a man's discontentment. Marriage is no longer centered on the husband's happiness; you have the right to seek out your own fulfillment and healthy life. Marriage thrives when the man and woman derive mutual fulfillment and joy sharing their lives. Be ready to admit your faults and failings, but don't forget that a marriage takes two: both you and your husband have a hand in the health of your marriage and are responsible for making it succeed.

CHAPTER 2:

AN AUTO OBSESSION

ZACK AND ELAINE'S
CAR CONUNDRUM

The room was dimly lit with a halo of light hovering around the computer. Three hours had come and gone, and it was now eleven o'clock at night. In just a few hours, it would be time to go to work, but he was in a zone and needed a little more time. His head was bowed, and his body was hunched over with excitement.

From the corner of Elaine's eye, she could see her husband and how lost he had already become within his favorite place and knew tonight would be like the countless others. Elaine was a beautiful girl with long legs that fit her frame perfectly. Every part of her complimented another part. She was, no doubt, a beautiful woman. Her husband, Zach, never seemed to notice her, though, because her name wasn't Betsy and she wasn't a '69 Mustang. That's all Zach talked about, his car, Betsy. Sometimes Elaine felt a real competition with Betsy; it felt as if Betsy were alive and an actual other woman. Some nights, just for fun, Elaine would dress skimpily and slide one leg across the car and seductively ask for some help from her husband. Zach never seemed to notice, though. He only had eyes for Betsy.

The alarm boomed in Elaine's ears. She groggily climbed out of the bed and soon realized that Zach wasn't in the bed. She knew exactly where he was; he was with Betsy. *Ugh, will this car never go away?* Elaine thought. It had only been three years since they got married, and everything had abruptly changed. The sensitive man who only wanted to do what she wanted to do was but a memory at this point and had been replaced with a car nut who couldn't keep himself away from the garage.

Feeling overwhelmed with confusion about her marriage and how to fix it, Elaine decided to call a marriage counselor. She wanted to get a hold of the problem that caused her husband's indifference toward her. She made an appointment with a therapist named Dr. Brown through the doctor's website. So many things went through Elaine's mind as she realized how much she loved her husband and how she truly wanted it to work. She just hoped that Dr. Brown would help her learn how.

Feeling challenged, and a little bit sleepy, Elaine gradually climbed back into bed. Elaine was not herself anymore, either. She had nearly forgotten that there was a time that she always wore makeup, had smooth shaven legs, and every hair on her head stayed in perfect position. Yes, she had begun to let herself go slowly…but that shouldn't matter, right?

UNDERSTANDING YOUR HUSBAND'S ENGINE ENTHUSIASM

For some men, anything with a powerful engine is just about the most enthralling thing they could imagine. While most women don't understand the attraction, if your husband has emotionally withdrawn from your relationship in order to direct his focus toward a vehicle, you are not alone.

While men often find the female mind and emotional intimacy perplexing, engines make more tangible, concrete sense. Working on a car, truck, or boat has long served as a respite for men under emotional stress. It's a puzzle they can solve.

As foolish as you may find the attraction, you will need to learn to respect it for its benefits before you confront your husband about the problems his new focus has created. The relief, calm, and clarity he most likely is drawn to in his mechanic work are clearly providing him something that is helping him cope with stress.

Learn to respect what this new challenge has given him so you don't begin your discussion with an accusation. He will likely feel personally threatened if you attack something that brings him so much enjoyment and comfort. Be ready to hear what he has been getting from his distraction so you can better understand why he feels he can't be emotionally present in your marriage.

HELPING HIM KICK THE HABIT

Your husband will have his own personal reasons for being drawn to a mechanical distraction. Likely, he is drawn to vehicles as a distraction because they present a puzzle that can be solved with learning and physical effort. The trial and error, diagnosis, and delicate handiwork that working on an engine require appeals to mechanic-minded men on many levels. It moves them from the abstract and subjective world of a complex relationship to the concrete and objective world of mechanics. An engine has certain parts that will always work the same way. A marriage is more intricate than that. You cannot just lift up the hood and listen to gauge the problem at hand.

Understanding what is behind the attraction to your husband's distraction will enable you to begin the process of getting to the source of your marital problems and start working toward a solution. If he is drawn by the easy-to-solve puzzle aspect of vehicles, he is likely feeling that he can never solve the riddles that come up in marriage. Many men are so confused by how and why women behave the way they do that they turn to easier-to-solve problems for relief.

You've probably heard most men complain about their wives: "I can't understand her anymore!"; "She has changed!"; "She is too complex for me!"; "Her emotions are wrecking our relationship!"

These are a few comments that reveal how clueless some men are when it comes to dealing with a female's emotional makeup.

> Likewise, ye husbands, dwell with them according to *knowledge*, giving honour unto the wife, as unto the weaker vessel, and as being heirs together of the grace of life; that your prayers be not hindered.
>
> 1 Peter 3:7 (KJV)

It takes hard work to understand how the mind of a woman works, and most men are not prepared to do this type of work because the job description changes many times in a day.

A man can also gravitate toward working on a vehicle because it is a project that he gets to work on alone. This solitude, combined with the act of working with his hands, can be a sort of therapy for a man. Because men are more likely to be kinetic learners than women, working with their hands can aid in relaxation and rejuvenation. Understanding your husband's newfound love for mechanics will set you on the right path when it comes to repairing your marriage.

Finding a way that makes your husband feel comfortable communicating is critical, as a lack of open communication is the root of the problem at hand. While women often find discussing their emotions easy and relieving, men usually find this kind of sharing too exposing for comfort. In fact, some men are so uncomfortable with this kind of perceived vulnerability that they learn how to block almost all emotion in order to maintain control of themselves.

HOMEWORK FOR YOUR MARRIAGE

Much of this work can be done by you and your husband in your own home. To remedy this problem on your own, you will need to feel secure in your commitment to each other and have equal levels of commitment to solving the conflict at hand. Read the following list to see if you are ready to tackle this marital issue by yourselves.

To succeed in overcoming your obstacles, both you and your husband must be ready, willing, and able to:

- Learn more effective communication methods
- Refrain from placing blame
- Discuss whenever possible and only argue when absolutely necessary
- Hear your partner's point of view
- Make concessions
- Stand up for your individual needs
- Prioritize mutual respect and conflict resolution over personal or prideful defenses
- Stick with this until its resolved

Sadly, most people do not have the above skills. You will, no doubt, pick some of them up as you trudge through your conflict-resolution process, but that's not the only option you have. Even if you feel you and your husband are capable of the things on this list, marriage counseling can make the process much less painful.

WHEN TO SEEK PROFESSIONAL HELP

There is no shame in attending marriage counseling sessions. These days, many pastors or priests require the couples they marry to participate in some amount of premarital counseling. Talk therapy has been proven to improve all relationships, including your relationship with yourself, and marriage therapy is just the same.

If you are unable to create a safe, calm space for you and your husband to tackle your marital problems, marriage counseling could drastically reduce your stress. Counseling will also increase the odds of you both getting what you want in the long run. But all marriage counselors or therapists are not the same. You must carefully choose a marriage counselor who meets your beliefs and expectations. A marriage therapist offers the third party opinion and mediation services that make conflict resolution much easier than when tackled alone.

CLOSING SOLUTION

In this chapter, you were able to understand a little more about why your husband may be spending more time in the garage than with you. The issue that we call the "other woman" in this chapter is a distraction by vehicle or machines to avoid communicating or the switch of focus to a task that is solved with physical effort from an issue that requires emotional openness or intimacy.

For some, sitting down with one another at the dining room table and talking openly is all it takes to get a marriage back on track. For others, however, this kind of openness is a bit more difficult. If you fall in the latter group, you will benefit most by seeking help from a counselor who will be able to both guide the discussion and offer an unbiased point of view.

Let's close out by peeking in on Zach and Elaine:

Elaine grabbed her purse and rushed out the front door. She was now on her way to the first therapy appointment with Dr. Brown. Elaine had made the appointment and then told Zach. Zach was hesitant, but Elaine had insisted that she really felt like she needed to talk things through with a therapist and wanted him to come as well. Zach agreed.

From Elaine's eyes:

Elaine hopped in the car and sped off. As she pulled into the parking lot, she saw Zach waiting for her. He was polishing his car while he waited. Elaine let out a sigh as she got out the car. She walked over, joined her husband, and they walked in together. They checked in and waited to be called. After a couple of minutes, they went back to see Dr. Brown. As they entered the room and sat down, Elaine felt a little relief. She would finally get a chance to express herself and hopefully understand Zach more.

From Zach's eyes:

Zach pulled into the parking lot of Dr. Brown's office. No Elaine. Zach was originally against coming in to see a therapist but over the last week had decided that maybe Elaine was right. Their marriage seemed to be a little strained lately. Zach parked the car, got out, and started wiping his car down in an attempt to calm his nerves before the counseling appointment that he was still a little apprehensive about. Zach smiled as Elaine pulled in. They went inside together. Zach felt a little nervous, but all his nerves were eased when he entered the room. This would be the beginning of a new start for them.

Though marriage therapy does not solve all marriage problems, it is usually one of the best ways to get started resolving several marital problems such as this one. Zach and Elaine undoubtedly found help to start rebuilding their strained relationship.

CHAPTER 3:

THE SEDUCTION
OF SPORTS

MICHAEL AND SELENA'S
NEAR STRIKE OUT

"Hey honey, can you please move to the side. Umm, a little farther left. Thank you, darling."

"Okay, can you see better now, Papi?" Selena asked in her thick Colombian accent.

Her hair fell to the middle of her back with glossy chocolate curls framing her petite silhouette. Selena was a spicy woman from Colombia with beautiful, sleepy eyes. She was standing in the middle living room wearing only Michael's oversized college tee shirt; he'd always found Selena irresistible when she was wearing nothing but one of his favorite tee shirts. She cocked her head to the side, watching Michael and waiting for a response.

"Yes, honey, that's great," Michael said. "How was your day?" he asked absentmindedly as he stared at the baseball game on the television.

Shaking her head, Selena tossed her flowing curls behind her back. She edged herself into his periphery in an attempt to grab his attention, but his eyes remained fixed on the TV screen. Finally, Selena gave up. She went into the room, threw on a pair of flannel pants, and plopped down to watch the baseball game with him. That night the Mets were playing the Browns.

Michael was a robust man who stood five foot eleven inches. He had intelligent blue eyes and was the definition of masculinity.

He was also a complete sports fanatic, so much so that he hadn't even noticed Selena's attempts to get attention because he was so focused on the game.

To the outsider looking in, Selena was the type of woman that no man could ignore. She was an independent sports commentator who was quietly confident and loudly attractive.

Selena was now sleeping, her head lying in Michael's lap. When the game was over, Michael gently picked her up and laid her in their bed. The room was dimly lit, which created a dreamy effect. He laid her down gently, and her robe slowly opened. A grin came to Michael's face; he was one lucky guy. Billie Holiday crooned softly in the background through the bedroom stereo speakers. Everything about the moment was sweet and sensual.

Just as Michael began to kiss Selena's exposed shoulder, he suddenly bolted from his wife's side to the next room with a sense of urgency that suggested the house was on fire. *The highlights!* he thought as he rushed to turn on the TV. It was now ten o' clock, and there was at least an hour of commentary left for him to watch before he had to go to bed. He opened the fridge, grabbed a soda, and settled down in front of their flat screen TV that had images of pop flies and almost-too-close-to-call plays racing cross it. *Ah, this was the life*, he thought to himself.

Selena woke up early the next morning and felt around the bed for her husband. Like usual, he wasn't there. Her plan had failed again. She was going to have to really step it up.

Selena wanted a child. She and her husband had been married for a little over a year now, and she was hoping for a child. She was twenty-six and had traveled all over the world doing sports commentary. She was now ready to focus on the home, settle down, and raise two children in a house that had a white picket fence. This wasn't going to be an easy sell for Selena, though. Michael was and always had been obsessed with sports; his life revolved around them. He even proposed to her during the seventh inning stretch. He got down on one knee, stared up at the scoreboard, and asked her to spend the rest of his life with him. It was comical and consistent; Michael was oblivious to anything but the sports he watched. That was one of the reasons she married him.

They shared a common interest in sports. Michael was a successful baseball trainer, and Selena, as mentioned, was a sports commentator. He had an MBA and possessed a subtle coolness that women adored. He only noticed one woman though, his Selena.

Unfortunately, Selena did have a rival, and she was known to most as America's favorite pastime. Selena was competing against baseball. . Michael had been having an affair with her for over ten years now. It was the running joke of the office that Selena had finally met a woman that was more attractive than she. The joke wasn't as funny as it had been previously, though, especially after what had happened last night. Well, tonight would be different.

It was five o'clock when Selena got home. She had managed to get off work early even though it was playoff season. She got home immediately, turned the TV on, and flipped over to the game while she got everything prepared. Although it was their anniversary, she knew they would not be going to a fancy restaurant because a fancy restaurant would not have a television. Michael would not be going to a place that deprived him of his beloved baseball, especially during the playoffs. She knew the man she married and was okay with who he was. Lately though, his obsession with sports was beginning to make her really consider her own generosity in the marriage.

Tonight she would prepare an anniversary meal since she knew restaurant reservations were out of the question. Selena quickly whipped up her special white sauce with peaches for the shark she had prepared. She had marinated shark, conch, and scallops together in a light seafood marinade, slowly cooking them in garlic, butter, onion, and cilantro. She was also baking her famous macaroni and cheese that Michael loved so much. For the finale, she would lightly blanch some asparagus tips.

Selena had thought of everything. The table was covered in white lace and sprinkled with rose petals. Everything was beautiful; a bottle of Michel was chilling in a bucket of ice on the table. *Oh, look at the time*, she thought. She was paying so much attention to detail, she had not realized how much time had passed.

Rushing, Selena climbed in her now lukewarm bath, unable to take the time she had planned. She had pulled it off, though. She dressed in a little black cocktail dress and was wearing the first pair of diamond earrings Michael had bought her. Her hair was flowing down like Michael liked it, her thick curls cascading down her back. Everything was perfect. "Okay," she said out loud, "everything looks amazing. Now all that's left is to wait for Michael to come home."

It was now seven o'clock. Each time she looked up, it grew later and later. She lost count of how many times she had called Michael. Seven became half past nine. It was obvious that Michael had forgotten their anniversary. Selena was tired, heartbroken, and too drained to eat. She decided to give him one more call.

The phone screamed in Michael's ear. What was wrong with Selena today? She had been calling nonstop. *I am mean, didn't she realize that tonight was the playoffs and the Mets had made it?* he thought to himself. When he had married her, what made her so attractive to him was her love for sports, but lately she seemed to be so distracted. "Ugh, there's my phone again," he said out loud and irritated. *That's it*, he thought. *I am going to shut it off. I can't hear the highlights from the game.* Michael had decided to go to a sports bar to celebrate the Mets making it to the playoffs. He was surrounded with his friends and baseball highlights. This was the happiest day of his life.

UNDERSTANDING YOUR HUSBAND'S LOVE FOR THE GAME

Whether your husband played football or golf in high school, sports are a huge part of many men's lives from elementary school until the day they die. Regardless of whether you share this passion or can relate to it, if your husband has become so overly engrossed in sports that your relationship is deteriorating, an intervention is needed. Do it for yourself, for him, and for your marriage.

The ways a person can become obsessed with sports to the point of distraction are varied. Different sports, different types of participating, and different kinds of fandom will depend on your husband's preferences.

Do you think you may have a sports problem in your marriage? The following is a list of known ways that people use sports to escape everyday life:

- Collecting baseball or other sports cards
- Online interactive strategy competitions like Fantasy Football
- Betting
- Excessive team fandom
- Obsessing over a particular athlete

An unhealthy level of distraction caused by sports is possible with any sport. In all these cases, regardless of the type of distraction or the specific sport, sports hobbies are clearly avoidant behaviors that keep your husband from dealing with the emotions that frighten him.

Because sports are so prevalent in our culture, it is easy to stay obsessed. With modern technology, anyone can, with just a few clicks, get updates about their favorite teams, players, and sports right on their cell phones. Being able to constantly reach out and access this information makes it easy for people to disappear into this distraction at any time wherever they are.

A LACK OF SPIRITUALITY

Another common reason people, and men in particular, are drawn to a sports team deals with the spiritual side of being human. Spirituality can also be very obsessive, but true spirituality from Christianity point of view can help one reorder his life appropriately and focus on what is essential in life. Every person is driven by a need to belong. Finding something like a sport is an accessible way for someone to develop a sense of belonging. The same type of belonging some people seek in fellowships, churches, clubs, temples, and societies. One may also find comfort in a group of avid friends who share an understanding and an opinion that binds them together.

Human beings find this comforting sense of identity in a number of ways. Sports are just one of the many things a person can disappear into in order to find a strong identity they can associate with.

The following is a brief list of other ways people find a sense of belonging or identity:

- Gender
- Ethnicity
- Family
- Neighborhood
- Nationality
- Class

- Religion
- Politics
- Gangs
- Social clubs
- Career

This desire to belong is not a bad thing; in fact, it is an essential and beautiful part of being human. The means by which we find comfort are neither positive nor negative. Instead, it is the level of commitment to the identity that can be negative; what we sacrifice to maintain our association with it and the way it affects our life as a whole.

In this case, an obsession with a sports team is probably positive for the husband in that it provides him a sense of belonging and purpose. On the other hand, it also is a negative because it is ruining his marriage. If this is the case for your husband, you'll need to convince him that investing his time in being a loving husband can be an equally enjoyable and fulfilling way to establish his unique identity.

HELPING HIM KICK THE HABIT

Whether it is life stress or fear of intimacy causing the trouble, helping your husband carefully face the strong feelings that are trapping him will restore your marriage. He will need to recognize what is driving him to his distractions. You can help him by calmly and clearly telling him the harm his lack of focus on your marriage is causing.

This kind of deep, personal introspection may not be possible without the help of counseling. Both marriage and individual therapy is useful in these cases, as you will likely need to address his relationship to himself and his own emotions, as well as his relationship and commitment to you.

Regardless of what works for you and your husband, make sure you let him know every step of the way that you are willing to support him. Most men have an incredibly deep-set fear of being seen as weak. This is one of the main reasons wives find their husbands running away from intimacy.

CLOSING SOLUTION

Have you thought, *When is the season over? When will they stop having Super Bowl on Sundays?* There are so many men who watch sports. Typically because the love for the sport, they become like dedicated players. However, it is detrimental when the sports games become more important than the time that he spends with you. There are many different ways to approach this issue. As his wife, you can make some compromises while making sure that he isn't avoiding dealing with an issue. If there is some avoidance, then counseling may be an option. But some compromises and communicating your feelings may just be the answer!

Let's look in on Selena and Michael.

Selena was still very hurt by Michael's forgetting their anniversary and ignoring her repeated phone calls. Michael had apologized for standing her up, but Selena was tired of his apologies. Michael needed to understand that she loved sports, especially baseball, too, but their marriage was her priority, and it should be his as well. She loved him and wanted to have time with him without competing with the TV. Selena had decided to sit down and talk with Michael about how she was feeling.

She got home early and knew she would have plenty of time to spend with him since it was Friday. Selena came in, laid out Chinese food on the table, and waited for Michael.

Michael walked through the door about five minutes later.

"Hmmm, what smells so good?" Michael said as he walked into the dining room.

"It's Chinese. Wash up, and let's eat. I have some things I want to talk about," Selena said sweetly with a smile.

Michael went and washed up and sat at the table. They chatted about their days, and then Selena began telling Michael that she had begun to feel she was second to his love for baseball. She said that she didn't mind doing things around baseball season, but she wanted him to think about her more. Michael listened intently, agreed that he was being a little obsessive, and admitted he didn't want to lose a marriage over baseball.

Selena and Michael agreed on a compromise that would allow him time for baseball and Selena. Michael particularly agreed to not watch all the highlights and give that time to Selena.

CHAPTER 4:

THE CONSUMING CAREER

JARED AND CINDY'S BIG CRUNCH

It was late, and Jared was going to miss his commuter, but he had just a little more to do. He had called his wife hours ago and told her he may be staying overnight again because he would miss his commuter. They lived in uptown New York, but he worked in Westchester. He often stayed late or overnight. In fact, he even had an overnight kit and blanket that stayed at the office.

Some of Jared's coworkers felt like his marriage was troubled because he was in the office so much. What they didn't understand was that he loved his work. He was a passionate man, but he reserved the bulk of his passion for numbers. Jared had been an accountant for over fifteen years. He graduated with an accounting BA from the University of New York. He viewed his work as an art form.

It was at the University of New York that Jared met Cindy Patterson, his wife now of ten years. Theirs was an interesting relationship that consisted of hellos and goodbyes. They had never really had an argument, and that was probably due to the fact that Jared was never around to argue with. Cindy was an accountant as well, but she worked for a different firm that was in uptown where they lived, and she moderated her time at the office.

When comparing the two careers, one would notice the difference in the couple's work by the different type of clientele they both had. Jared's clientele was more businesses accounting needs while hers were the social elite. Although Cindy loved her work, she was grounded and able to leave the office at a decent hour every day. Cindy could detach herself from accounting to experience life outside of work. If you were to compare the level of competency each had within their careers, it was obvious that Cindy was just as brilliant as her husband; however, she was not as devoted to numbers.

Jared was often reclusive and became euphoric when solving unexplained tax problems for his business clients. He was described best as a workaholic by all of his coworkers. Jared had an average life that could be extraordinary if he just looked at the blessings around him. He and his wife had an excellent income; they had no children and were already prepared for retirement at the age of thirty-nine. There was absolutely nothing to run from in Jared's life.

Above all other aspects of Jared's life, he was lucky in that he was married to a woman who seemed tailor-made for him. Jared and Cindy were uniquely suited for each other, as they shared the same interests and passions. The only thing separating them from a near-perfect life was the fact that Jared was a workaholic and never had time for his wife. While Cindy was fast asleep at home, Jared would be up at his office crunching numbers.

It was five in the morning, and the sun had not yet come up. Cindy was thinking about all that she needed to do for the day and realistically how much she would be able to accomplish. She was a driven woman, but she always felt like she was not getting enough R&R. She had been getting calls a lot lately, but it was just too early to think about that just yet. She had to hop in the shower and get ready.

Freshly showered and pouring herself a cup of coffee, she was finally alone with her thoughts. The sound of the toaster startled her. The echo in their massive home always seems to unnerve her because, outside of their cat Nancy, it was always just her in the house. Cindy stood in her kitchen, quiet and thinking, as she nibbled on her morning toast. She absentmindedly petted Nancy as she gazed blankly ahead and let her mind wander. Still left in her musings, she wondered what her husband was up to. Instead of wondering, she decided to call.

The high-pitched ring of the phone in his empty office startled Jared, causing him to knock over last night's coffee. Luckily for him, the coffee just missed his papers and poured onto the floor. The coffee remained in a brown puddle on the floor and took its place among the several other coffee stains that were born from similar incidents. Jared's marriage wasn't the only thing suffering from his long office hours; his carpet had taken some abuse as well. Picking up the phone, Jared answered, "Yes?"

Cindy was used to the gruffness of his voice in the morning and completely ignored his Al Bundy tone. She proceeded to ask her husband how his night was. He told her that it was great. He began to immediately ramble on about his work and never once asked her about herself or how her day was.

"I'm telling you, honey, these type of write-offs only happen once in a lifetime." Jared was raving about another loophole he had found and how much it was going to help his client. As he talked, his eyes would light up, making him almost handsome. His little balding head would glisten with perspiration when he talked about accounting. He continued rambling on.

Finally, Cindy broke into the conversation, "Well, Jared, I have to go." She was blunt, and her voice was a little chilly.

Startled and thrown out of his trance, he said, "Okay." The zeal that hung on every word when he was talking about numbers had faded, and his voice returned to its monotone norm as soon as his wife interrupted his tirade.

Cindy, relieved to get off the phone, quickly took the last bite of her toast. Their relationship may have seemed strange, but she was used to it. She had never known anything different. This was as good as it got. She accepted the fact years ago that she was married to a man who was married to his work.

UNDERSTANDING YOUR HUSBAND'S PREOCCUPATION WITH OCCUPATION

For as long as modern marriage has been around, men have been burying themselves in their careers as a way to escape whatever they fear at home. Today, women sometimes pull the same trick by thoroughly engrossing themselves in their career in order to avoid the vulnerability of marriage. While this is an age-old escape, it still destroys many a marriage.

Career success is, of course, something that just about everyone wants. When discussing the issue of too much work and too little focus on the marriage with your husband, he may complain that you are implying he should put his career on the backburner.

This is another situation in which you need to communicate calmly and clearly the line that divides healthy professional drive from obsession and avoidance. Work is an inevitable part of man's existence, but when work becomes a replacement for marital intimacy, then a frank discussion between you and your husband is urgently needed. If you deduce that he works to finance a wired dream, let him know what the wise man King Solomon said: "I have seen all the works which have been done under the sun, and behold, all is vanity and striving after wind" (Ecclesiastes 1:14, NASB).

CLARIFYING THE CONFLICT

The line that divides obsession from healthy enthusiasm is less clear when it comes to repairing your marriage after your husband has become too distracted by his career. You will both need to sit down and analyze your shared goals.

The following questions are a great way to start a conversation with your husband:

- What is it that you want for your shared future?
- Are you on the same page regarding what career level you are each aiming for?
- Are you both equally committed to the sacrifices reaching that ideal career level will require?
- Which of your needs aren't being met because of your husband's current level of commitment to his career?

HELPING HIM KICK THE HABIT

Sometimes, especially when the husband is the main moneymaker, men bury themselves in their careers as a way to balance the stress of not having enough money to provide what they believe is necessary. Often, discussing openly together what your shared priorities are will help your husband realize that he doesn't need to be working so hard.

If, on the other hand, it comes to light that your husband is truly running from your marriage by hiding in his career, the discussion that needs to take place will be slightly different. Rather than tackling stress-inducing financial issues, you will need to broach the subject of what keeps him from connecting with you. It is important for you to understand what it is he is running from when he buries himself in his work and career advancement.

CLOSING SOLUTION

It is hard in a fast-paced society to determine what necessary overtime work is and what is workaholic behavior. Many times, passion for a career can turn into an obsession.

There are so many demands on employees that it can be easy to slip into a position in which a person spends more time with an employer than with family. Your husband may have the tendency to become a workaholic, and, because of that, he has spent more and more time away. It is important to acknowledge your husband's seemingly over-the-top dedication to his career and discuss the reasons he works so much. Sometimes, just bringing the issue to his attention may change things over time. If your husband does have a tendency to obsess over his work though, it will take some self-discipline to change. If your issues prove to be a little more complicated, however, it is definitely time to seek professional help from a counselor.

Let's catch up with Jared and Cindy and see what they did.

Jared wrapped up everything at work early. Cindy had called and said that they needed to have a serious conversation about their marriage. Jared was slightly nervous. He was afraid she wanted a divorce. He knew he hadn't always been around, but he loved her and couldn't imagine being with anyone else.

Jared made it down to the train and hopped on. As he sat on the train ride home, he was almost certain she wanted to discuss his being away so much. Jared wanted to slow down at times, too, but just couldn't stop working. He had financially achieved more than he imagined in such a short amount of time. Now he just needed to focus on coming home to Cindy.

What Jared never shared with his wife was that he was a little afraid to come home because he didn't really know her anymore and had some fear that she wouldn't like him as much if he were around. The train came to a halt at his stop, and he got off. To his surprise, Cindy was waiting for him there. She had driven her car over. They got into the car together and headed to their house where she had secretly prepared for an evening of romance. They were silent the entire car ride home. There was an almost tangible tension. As they pulled into the driveway, Jared broke into a cold sweat.

Without knowing how else to deal with the situation or his nervous energy, Jared spit out, "Is this going to take long? I brought some work with me." Jared swallowed back his own shock and regret from what he had just said. He didn't mean to say that. He had brought work home so he could be with her a few days.

Cindy was infuriated with what she just heard. She got out of the car and slammed the door. Jared jumped out and followed her quickly, stuttering and stumbling over himself the whole way inside. Huffing and puffing, Jared caught up as she was fumbling for the keys to open the door.

Jared grabbed her and squeezed her tightly in a loving embrace. He told her he was sorry. He was nervous about the night and that just came out. He actually was home for a few days and only brought work for that reason. As he spoke, he could feel her body trembling and her chest rising and falling in an almost rhythmic way. Tears were streaming down her face. As Jared stood explaining himself, her anger faded into relief and her relief into elation. He did love her and cared about their marriage.

Cindy and Jared went inside and talked, ate, and talked some more. They discussed things other than work and laughed together. Cindy lovingly explained her fears and complaints with Jared's work habits. Jared sat and really listened to what his wife had to say. They both opened up. After years of living one way, they began to find the benefits of really talking and developing intimacy, not just dependency, in a relationship. There is more to a marriage than just trusting that the other knew that he or she was loved. That evening they began to develop a genuine closeness that transformed their marriage from a partnership to an affectionate relationship. They went on to share a night together that was better than their honeymoon.

CHAPTER 5:

THE HAZARD OF HOBBIES

CHRIS AND MAGGIE'S
PRECARIOUS PASTIMES

There was no place that Chris wouldn't go for the perfect photo. He had spent his lifework traveling to different places and becoming completely engrossed in his environment in an attempt to capture a masterpiece on film. Currently he was climbing up his personal Mount Everest, the Topanga Canyon. He was beginning to feel achy; he wasn't as young as he used to be. He leaned over and began to stretch.

"Whew, nothing like a good stretch in between an intense climb," Chris said to his wife, Maggie. (Although she couldn't make it, he still talked to her on the phone. It was beginning to get dark, and the sun was setting.)

"Hey, Mag Pie, you should see it."

Maggie stayed on the phone talking to her husband and listening to his travel stories until she realized that it was almost time for her date. Maggie had been seeing someone behind Chris's back for the last three months and was considering leaving him. In her eyes, she ranked last to his hobbies and outdoor adventures. In fact, it had been five years since they were even on a vacation together. They still traveled and took vacations, but now they did so alone, or Chris did so alone, anyway. Although they took separate vacations, Maggie was not always taking lone vacations. Michael, the man Maggie was currently seeing, had been on the last two.

"Okay, babe! Got to go," Maggie said in one hurried breath, trying to get off the phone before Michael arrived. She had been staring at her watch the entire time Chris had been rambling about the scenery. She had heard the same thing every time he was on a trip tackling the great outdoors and had lost her interest in the one-sided conversations in which Chris gave detailed accounts of everything he saw and how it made him feel without ever even pausing for Maggie's input long ago. She just wanted to get through the phone call so she could start her evening with Michael. He had a surprise for her tonight, and it was all she could think about. If Chris noticed his wife's inattention on the other end of the phone, he didn't seem to show any signs.

When the two hung up, he stared out at the trees reverently and thought, *This is exactly where I want to be.*

There were five things Chris never left home without: gear for hiking, food, water, camera, and his mobile tent. Sometimes after a good hike, he would set up his tent and stay the night. He never thought about how his wife might feel being left at home alone so often. He took her for granted and never dreamed that she would leave him. He was so wrapped up in his love for the outdoors and photography that he had failed to notice his wife was drifting away.

Maggie had always been his opposite. She had pretended to like the outdoors to snag him, but the truth was, she could care less about spending time with nature. If there wasn't tanning, a spa, and a nail salon close by, she wasn't interested. Although they were completely different, she had done everything she could to win Chris over. She had fallen in love with him when he came into the tanning salon she owned. He was quiet, reserved, and amazingly handsome; that was enough to pretend to like nature for a while.

While getting to know Chris, Maggie came to the conclusion that he was the strong, silent type. She had no idea he was just self-absorbed. Along with being self-centered, he was unhealthily attached to his mother and, until her death the previous year, would call her every day. He even called her while they were on their honeymoon. She hated to say it, but it was kind of a relief when that sweet, controlling, old lady passed.

Chris's mother, Mrs. Johnson, was from old money, and she treated anyone who wasn't born with a silver spoon in his or her mouth as inferior. When she first met Maggie, she had called her a stripper, with her orange skin, platinum blonde hair, and less than conservative clothing. Maggie wasn't fazed by Mrs. Johnson's offensiveness, however, because she had grown up with her aunt who happened to be a successful and very materialistic real estate agent. Any nastiness that old lady could dish out, she could take. Yes, Maggie could handle anything that was thrown her way. A big part of Maggie's high tolerance for insolence rested in the fact that her childhood had not been what one might call picture perfect, or even decent, really. Now that she was an adult and able to make her own decisions without criticism or consequence, she was ready to finally enjoy life. Unfortunately, Chris was not the kind of fun whom Maggie was looking for. He was consumed with nature and photography, both of which she found absolutely mind-numbing. The more she had gotten to know her husband over the years, the more boring he seemed to become to her. Chris's obsession with nature, coupled with the fact that he never once made an attempt to do anything Maggie was interested in, made Maggie feel like there would be no way to make her marriage work.

It was the morning of December 23, the day before Christmas Eve. Every year around this time, Chris would dart from store to store, rushing to find a Christmas gift for his wife. Of course, he had the entire year to plan, look for, and buy the perfect Christmas gift, or at the very least one that Maggie would actually like, but that was typical of Chris. His world revolved around his photography, and he just couldn't be bothered with taking time out of his packed schedule to do anything thoughtful for his wife of ten years. He had, however, purchased many gifts for his camera, which he lovingly named Lacey—new lenses,

attachments, even a studio. He had been purchasing items for
Lacey weeks ago, the last part of which were arriving today. He
may not have had time to think of his wife's birthday or what
she may really wanted for Christmas, but he never walked past
a camera store or flipped through a B&W magazine without
seeing something that would be perfect for Lacy.

On the other side of town, Maggie was picking up wrapping
paper for Michael and Chris's gifts. She knew that Chris had just
bought a new camera and had bought all the equipment that he
needed, which meant she bought him a bunch of expensive stuff
that was just like the other really expensive stuff that he already
had, only newer and slightly more advanced. Maggie never
understood what the point was in buying all this equipment
brand new year after year, but she knew it made Chris happy, so
she always did it. At one point, she even researched the cameras
as Chris bought them and perused photo magazine articles to
find out what the best brands were and what kind of equipment
worked best with the camera that he had. She still bought the
equipment for him, but she had stopped putting so much effort
into it after two Christmases ago when Chris found everything
he could have dreamed of for his camera nicely wrapped and
waiting for him under the Christmas tree, and Maggie found a
pair of slippers (that weren't even her size) and a bottle of perfume
that was his mother's favorite. That day Maggie began to realize
that there was something very off kilter about their relationship.

It was a Friday, and Chris would be home later on in the
evening, so Michael was going to come over early in the afternoon.
Today was D-day; she was going to finally decide whether she was
going to stay in her marriage or divorce her husband. There were
so many things about Chris that she realized she wasn't attracted
to: his obsession with his hobbies, the strange relationship he had
with his mother, his inability to think of someone besides himself.
Of course, there were redeeming qualities in her husband as well,
little things that made her love him, even when she may not have

liked him. She didn't know, though, if the little charming things were enough to eclipse his faults anymore, though.

UNDERSTANDING YOUR HUSBAND'S RECREATION FASCINATION

Whether it means having to have the latest and greatest technology or becoming obsessed with a social cause, hobbies are an easy way for either spouse to emotionally withdraw from a marriage. If your husband's new passion is putting you in second place, you need to bring this issue to his attention.

Hobbies and recreational activities, just like an interest in finance or cars, are not inherently destructive. In fact, they are almost always a healthy, useful way of relieving stress and exercising the brain. A problem only arises when stress causes a person to retreat into the safety of a hobby and the hobby becomes an escape. Understanding the difference between a healthy curiosity or passion and an obsession or distraction is paramount to bringing your husband back into your life emotionally.

The following list is made up of activities that many people, particularly men, become deeply fixated with during times of stress. Remember, every person has his or her own preferred coping skills, though, and your husband's may not be on the following list.

- Massive, multiplayer online games
- Console video games
- Collecting sports cards
- Science Fiction fandom
- Working out

It is important to keep in mind that it is the behavior associated with the hobby rather than the hobby itself that presents a problem. An interest in any of the above does not necessarily indicate a serious issue. Use your own judgment when discerning between an interest and an obsession.

THE FEAR OF CONNECTION

Men hide in their hobbies both consciously and subconsciously to avoid the intimacy their marriage requires. Sometimes the intimacy they shrink away from is merely the act of coming home to the same person day after day with expectations of sharing something as simple as exchanges on how the day was or what the plans for the weekend are. Men can be solitary and may, at times, feel claustrophobic in relationships that require them to give so much of themselves constantly. The emotion behind the commitment of marriage can be overwhelming to someone uncomfortable with sentimentality. It can be hard for a man to know how to appropriately react to strong feelings. Try to keep this in mind when explaining to your husband that you feel he has withdrawn for no reason.

When approaching your husband about intimacy concerns, always consider the level of sensitivity that *your* husband is comfortable dealing with to ensure you have a productive discussion. He has, most likely, worked to guard himself from vulnerability, so he may be terrified by the smallest of intimacies within your marriage. Don't let your frustration cloud your intentions with your husband, and always bear in mind that it is patience above all else that he needs from you while he learns how to deal with his emotions and your relationship in a healthy way that will benefit both of you and your marriage.

Your husband needs to know that you are willing to hear him without judgment before he will be ready to open up. This is true for everyone. No one would confess their innermost thoughts and fears to someone they weren't entirely confident would respect what they had to say. For many men, the true difficulty lies in trusting that once they have opened up, they will not be viewed as weak or less masculine for doing so. Because such a foundation of trust and confidence must be built to bring your husband to the point of open communication, be sure that you don't jeopardize what you've worked so hard to establish by reacting harshly to your husband's honesty. Always listen with an open mind and a loving heart.

CLOSING SOLUTION

Never say that your husband is unwilling to change until you have sat down with him and had a discussion in which you have approached the subject clearly, calmly, and with a willingness to listen to his side. Sometimes, all your husband may need is candor. Don't assume that he is aware of your feelings and consciously ignoring them; explain to him why you are feeling neglected. If you feel he is spending more time away from home concentrating on hobbies and recreational activities, let him know that you would like more time spent together or a renewed commitment to intimacy. Show him from Scriptures that "there is an appointed time for everything. And there is a time for every event under heaven" (Ecclesiastes 3:1, NASB).

Many men will become deeply engrossed in a hobby without even realizing that it is causing strife for his friends, family, and wife. This is because men focus with a one-track mind. They also usually need less emotionally connected time with their loved ones than women do. It is important to first make the distinction in what purpose a hobby or activity is serving; is his distraction caused by innocent oblivion, or is he using it to avoid handling everyday stress and intimacy?

Peeking back into Chris and Maggie's situation, we will see if she decided to call it quits after ten years of trying or give Chris another chance:

Chris was excited to see Maggie when he got home that night. She had no clue that he had actually gotten her something for Christmas months ago. He could not wait to see her reaction when she opened her diamond necklace and saw the two tickets to her favorite place, the Bahamas!

After speaking with Chris on the phone that afternoon, Maggie decided not to have the divorce discussion that evening. Chris seemed excited to be back home with her, so she wanted to give her marriage one last try. Maggie pulled into the driveway and was greeted by a candle-lit driveway. Chris had lined both sides of their drive with candles to welcome his wife home. As she approached the house, Chris opened the door. Maggie saw that he was clean cut and shaven. Chris wrapped his arms around her waist and pressed his lips to hers in a way he hadn't since their wedding night. She saw that the floor was covered with rose petals that led into the dining room where dinner awaited. Maggie was overwhelmed with Chris's thoughtfulness and on the verge of tears. She was completely taken by surprise.

After dinner, Chris rushed Maggie into the formal dining room where her two gifts, hand wrapped by Chris, laid waiting under the tree. His eyes flashed with excitement as he handed the gifts to his wife. Maggie burst into tears and began telling Chris about her affair with Michael and everything she had been feeling lately. Chris was stunned but felt like it was a wake-up call to him. He had not given his wife the attention she needed. As they talked and cried, the evening turned to night. Chris realized that he had a lot of work to do to be sure his wife was his priority, and Maggie realized that, although she had betrayed Chris's trust in response to his neglect, she also had a lot of work to do to regain his trust. They came to the conclusion that what they needed was a fresh start and a new line of open communication in which they shared, gave, and took in their marriage. They spent the rest of the weekend resolved to make their marriage work and in each other's arms.

CHAPTER 6:

THE MISTRESS NAMED MONEY

SAMSON AND SIRI'S INVESTMENT INTERRUPTION

Samson was a young man that was driven by financial success. Ever since Samson was a young boy, he was motivated by money. He was only in his midthirties, already owned several businesses, and was always looking for the next opportunity. Samson's entire life revolved around his business ventures; he never stopped working.

Samson had been focused on his career path his entire life. He was from Argentina, had moved to the United States for school, and settled here after an internship because he saw too much opportunity to leave. His family back home was distraught when he informed them that he was going to stay in the United States, but everyone who knew him could've guessed that, if he found any kind of opportunity in the United States, he wouldn't be returning. The drive to make money seemed to be a part of Samson's DNA.

Samson's plane landed, and the second he hit the ground, he was thinking about the meeting he had in less than an hour. He had been gone for two weeks and was still on the road. One of his businesses was about to buy out a major corporation, so he would have to be there to be sure everything was going as planned. Of course, he missed his wife, but his drive to succeed kept him away constantly, jumping from meeting to meeting and from city to city nonstop. That was a price he was willing to pay to make it in the business world, though. *This is for her, too,* he would think, trying to justify his continuous absence. Samson was running on schedule and decided to call his wife, Siri, while he was driving. He dialed her cell phone.

"Hello, honey," his wife answered with excitement in her voice. No matter how often he was gone, she always missed her husband and was eager for him to return from a business trip.

"Hello, baby. How are you doing this morning?" Samson replied sweetly.

"I'm fine. I was just getting ready to head into the store to check in. After that I was thinking about looking around at a new place to open up a second store," Siri said quickly, knowing that her husband never had too much time to chat.

"Great! Two stores mean twice the profit. I think we are on track financially to invest in a third location if things go as planned. What do you think?" Samson was a business partner now, not a husband who had been gone for two weeks and ready to see is wife.

"That sounds great," Siri replied with a little disappointment in her voice. "So when are you going to be home? I miss you and would love to spend some time together. I was thinking we might do a mini getaway."

"Well, I am hoping to return this week, but there is so much to do. We can take all the vacations we want after we hit our financial goals for this year. I don't want to get out of a good streak." Samson kept his business tone intact as he talked. "Well, I'm at the office now. I've got to run, sweetie. Talk to you later today."

"Bye," Siri said softly.

Samson hung up the phone, parked his rental car, and grabbed his briefcase and suit jacket from the back seat. He briefly looked up at the large corporate building that he was about to enter. In just a few hours, this would all be his. He smiled as he entered the building and let the receptionist know he was there for a meeting. She led him back to the main conference room. He placed his hand on the door and swung it open. He was stepping into his element.

Siri hung up the phone. She was a little upset that her husband didn't even consider her suggestion of getting away to spend a little time together. She needed to get away and relax. Siri had just found out that she was pregnant and wanted to take a vacation with her husband while they had the opportunity to just take off without months of planning and coordinating a babysitter. They had a small window in which they were free to do as they pleased now that Siri's younger sister, who she'd been raising since the death of her parents, was off to college and it was just the two of them.

Above all else, Siri just wanted some time with her husband before preparing for a baby. Siri sat and began to realize something huge: if Samson's focal point remained his business life, who was going to help through this pregnancy? Better yet, who would be there to help raise a child?

Siri never realized how consumed Samson was with money. She had actually married Samson because of his ambition and love to succeed. She saw his commitment as an admirable trait; he was just a man with goals who was willing to work hard to achieve them. She never knew how obsessive it would be. What she once saw as an asset, she began to view as a liability.

Siri was now eight weeks pregnant and starting to feel sick all the time. She was slender, so she would probably start to show soon. If she wouldn't be able to tell him on a couple's vacation, then she would need to go ahead and let Samson know as soon as he got home. The sooner she told him, the more time he would have to prepare financially for the baby's arrival. Siri knew that would be his first concern upon learning he was going to be a father.

Samson walked out of the meeting after four hours of negotiations. He not only owned this building but the other six locations! He bought the entire corporation and the entire sister companies. This meant he would be traveling for at least two more weeks. He would need to go to each of the new locations and begin the conversion process with all the managers. Depending on how everything went, he could be traveling for as long as a month. He knew Siri would probably be disappointed, but it was for her future, too, so she would have to understand.

Excited to tell her the good news, Samson called Siri immediately on leaving the meeting. When she answered, he didn't even let her say anything.

"Honey, I bought the entire corporation and have seven locations all together. We will definitely hit our goals for the year now! I will be traveling for at least two more weeks to get all the other locations on track. Maybe you can fly out to one of the locations so you can see what our future looks like! Wow, this is such a blessing!" Samson hadn't taken a breath yet.

"Great," Siri replied flatly. "I need to tell you something though. I was hoping to get to see you and talk with you, but there never seems to be a good moment, so here it is. I'm pregnant…"

UNDERSTANDING YOUR HUSBAND'S FINANCE FANATICISM

Is your husband obsessed with a love for money or worried about financial security? Whether you're just making rent each month or successfully investing thousands of dollars, finance and financial matters often become a shelter for men unable to face the conflicts and struggles in their marriage. Becoming illustrious in business is not wrong, but the obsessive pursuit of money for what it is can be very dangerous.

> If we have food and covering, with these we shall be content. But those who want to get rich fall into temptation and a snare and many foolish and harmful desires which plunge men into ruin and destruction. For the love of money is a root of all sorts of evil, and some by longing for it have wandered away from the faith and pierced themselves with many griefs.
>
> 1 Timothy 6: 8-10 (NASB)

There is a line between being smart with money and using finances to hide from emotional intimacy. The following are a list of questions to answer in order to find out whether your husband has a healthy, helpful interest and passion for finances or if is using it as an escape.

- Does he choose superfluous financial activities over spending time with you or his children?
- Do his interests and activities go beyond securing financial stability for you and your family?
- Does he place more importance on his financial pursuits than he does on spending time together?
- Has he actively turned you away in order to keep working on his current money making project?

These are all signs that your husband is attempting to dodge what he feels may be portrayed as vulnerability by hiding behind the all-encompassing world of finances. If his obsessive stock market updates and extensive spreadsheets are taking more from your relationship than they are adding, it's time to confront him about this distraction. A successful, healthy marriage requires both partners to actively engage in communication and the relationship works that are required. This means that if one person is devoting all of his or her energy to something like financial success, a marriage cannot operate the way it is supposed to.

Money is not just an idea; it is possessive and has a controlling influence. Scriptures call money Mammon, placing it in the realm of obsessive demonic spirits. The substance we call money is good, but the reckless pursuit and love of it is the root of so many evils and many marriages have been destroyed because the couple failed to see money for what it is: a tool, not our master.

HELPING HIM KICK THE HABIT

If your husband's intellectual attachment to financial pursuit is interfering with your marriage, you need to confront him about the problem in a loving manner. Avoid blaming, shaming, or using guilt as methods of approaching the subject, as this will only exacerbate the issue and push your husband further away.

Because an obsession with financial security is easy to disguise as smart money management, noticing exact obsessive behaviors is key to pointing out the legitimacy of your complaint. If your husband responds to your concerns by claiming he is merely trying to consolidate your financial stability, be ready to point out the flaws in his logic.

Remember to approach this topic delicately. If your husband is finding respite in his financial dealings, pointing out that his coping mechanism is creating problems in your marriage could put him on the defense. Be sure you have given yourself time for reflection before you enter into a discussion with your husband about what is going on. The atmosphere that you create will determine the success you will achieve in attempting to get your husband to change his focus from the bank account to your relationship.

CLOSING SOLUTION

Financial disagreements are extremely common within relationships, but they can be an indicator of something larger that lies just below the surface. There are many couples that have financial strain in their marriage, and that strain can ultimately lead to divorce if not handled correctly. Financial issues are still one of the leading causes of divorce. Because financial disagreements can be so damaging to a relationship, it is vital to address the problem in a straightforward but affectionate manner. Be clear, but not overbearing, when engaging in a dialogue with your husband about the concerns his money-mania is causing.

One often overlooked financial strain is found in the couple who does well financially, but one is more driven than the other in regards to the finances. This overzealous spouse becomes obsessed with financial success or ignores his wife or family in pursuit of it. This is not healthy.

If your husband seems to fit the description of a fanatical financier or moneymaking monster, he may also be reacting to his childhood experiences. Those who were raised in a household in which there was a constant lack of money will sometimes respond by being overly diligent with their own financial pursuits and fixated with their financial standing.

When discussing a possible problem in the marriage rooted in monetary obsession, understand and discuss what it is that is really driving your husband to the point of preoccupation, then be willing to listen and not hold grudges.

Let's look and see what is happening with Samson and Siri:

Samson was on his way to the airport. He was finally going home to his now pregnant wife! He was excited about becoming a dad. He knew it would be important to have everything financially ready, and this last business deal would ensure that they were absolutely set to have a child. The timing could not be more perfect.

During the last conversation that Samson and Siri had, he could hear the frustration in his wife's voice when she told him that they were expecting. He knew exactly why his wife was perturbed. She didn't want to tell him such life-changing news over the phone. She wanted the occasion to be special; she wanted it to be in person on a romantic vacation. He picked up his phone, dialed his travel agent, and had the agent start looking into last-minute weekend getaways that were available so he could take his wife on the couple's retreat she deserved. They were, after all, only going to have seven more months of alone time.

Siri was beyond herself when Samson came home with two tickets to an all-inclusive resort in Cozumel.

Before they left for their trip, Siri felt that she needed to get her concerns about her husband's money obsession out in the open. She didn't want to have the issue biting at her during the long-awaited getaway. As they were packing their luggage, Siri stopped and looked up at her husband.

"I need to talk to you about something, sweetheart," Siri said with a little uncertainty in her voice.

"Absolutely! You've got my full attention. Hit me," Samson replied, standing in front of the chest of drawers.

"I want to start by telling you that I am so proud of how much you've accomplished," Siri started. "But I have to say, babe, I sometimes worry about how involved you're going to be with our family. I can't do this by myself. I don't want to do it by myself. I need you to focus on us as much as you do the bank account."

Siri held her breath and waited for her husband's response.

"Honey," Samson said as he scooted the sundresses and swimsuits to the side and sat beside his wife, "you are absolutely right."

Siri sat, a little shocked, and asked, "I am?"

"Of course you are," Samson replied as he slipped his arm around his wife's shoulder. "I know that I get caught up in business and our investments. I want to be your husband and this little guy or girl's dad first, though, and a business tycoon second, and I will do whatever it takes to do that."

"Even if it means counseling?" Siri asked with apprehension. She knew that this was asking a lot.

"Even if it means counseling," Samson replied. "Now let's finish packing. We've got a honeymoon to revisit before junior arrives."

Samson had given the implementation tasks to his VP and wouldn't need to travel again for at least three weeks. They had doctor's appointments to go to, a bedroom to paint, and a nursery to furnish before he could even think about going out on the road again.

CHAPTER 7:

FOREVER FRAT: DISTRACTED BY FRIENDSHIPS

ELIZABETH AND STEVE'S BUDDY DEBACLE

L aughter was audible through the halls.
"Man, the only reason you are still here is because I saved you, man. I totally stepped in and gave you an olive branch," a big brother named Andre was telling his good buddy Steve.

They were at 1718 South Juniper Street Apt C, and Steve was having another poker night with the guys. The table was covered with beer cans, a bottle of vodka, popcorn, poker chips, and, of course, playing cards. Steve was a firm believer that friends always came before relationships. Friends were forever; girls come and go.

Unfortunately, no one ever warned Elizabeth about Steve's dedication to guy time before they exchanged their vows. Steve never seemed to be alone. He was always hanging out with someone and doing something. There were basketball Sundays, poker Tuesdays, golf Saturdays, and that didn't even count every night a sporting event was on that required a get-together at his favorite sports bar. Although Elizabeth probably should've realized long ago that her husband had a lifelong membership to the He-Man Women Haters Club, she seemed to fail to realize that there was a real issue there or she failed to realize how that issue would affect her life in the long run. Now that she was married to someone who always put her second, however, she was really starting to see the problems that Steve's dedication to the dudes were causing. Yes, Steve and his buddy time was a lot to for a marriage to handle, and it wasn't just the excessive level of camaraderie that created turbulence in Steve and Elizabeth's relationship. Not only did Steve spend 90 percent of his waking time with his pals, he told them every intimate detail about his and Elizabeth's personal life. Elizabeth knew that she couldn't share a private moment with her husband, and that was quite a concern, as marriage was supposed to be established on trust and intimacy. Every personal incident Elizabeth ever shared with Steve, regardless of how delicate or embarrassing it may have been, Steve would recount to his buddies as they were sitting around playing video games or watching a fight on TV. Steve's friends knew as much about his wife as he did.

Elizabeth had sat down with Steve in the past and told him that he had crossed lines with his inability to keep private matters private. He had nothing to say in response. As Elizabeth tried to address a serious problem in their marriage, Steve's fingers flew across his phone's screen as he mass texted his friends that his wife wouldn't stop nagging him to keep her embarrassing stories a secret. He didn't seem to appreciate the gravity of the situation. Steve seemed oblivious to how his wife was feeling. He couldn't understand what the big deal was if he liked to hang out with his friends and he was open with them about the stuff that he and Elizabeth shared. *I have the best friends in the world in Andre, Vince, and Mike*, Steve would think as he considered why his wife was so mad. *Why does she want to come between me and my friends?*

Steve was and always would be faithful to his fraternity brothers and his old high school friends; they were who mattered to him. He didn't know if his marriage would make it, but that wasn't a major concern for him. As long as he had his friends, he could make it through anything.

UNDERSTANDING YOUR HUSBAND'S BROTHERLY BONDS

When a man seems to spend more time with his friends than he does at home with his family, it can be hard for his wife to feel like she has solid ground to base her complaint on. Friendship is a good thing, after all. How can anyone rightly complain about this basic and important social aspect of living a happy and healthy life?

It is healthy and beneficial for men and women alike to have a group of friends to support, entertain, and encourage them throughout life's trials and triumphs. However, when a marriage commitment is made, both parties need to be ready to prioritize their partner over friends and family. That is the level of commitment that makes marriage as continually significant as it is.

It is distressing to realize that our society often portrays women who are standing up for themselves within their marriage as whiney, needy, or boring. Don't let this stereotype stop you from asking for the attention and energy you deserve from your husband. If you feel your husband ignores you in order to spend more time with his friends, you deserve some explanation. It is his duty now to be your partner and honor the commitment he made to you the day you both vowed till death do you part. When he made the decision to share his life with you, he made the decision to always consider you before all others. If he isn't living up to his end of the bargain, you are well within your rights to address the problem at hand.

SELF-REFLECTION: MAKING SURE HE IS THE PROBLEM

All that being said, there is a caveat that is occasionally applicable to these situations. No one wants to admit that they may be part of the problem, but without that sort of honest self-reflection and willingness to admit weakness, a truly communicative relationship is not possible. Before sitting down with your husband to discuss the ways he needs to work harder in your marriage, be sure you have considered the problem from all angles.

If, after thought and reflection, you come to the conclusion that the above situation mirrors your own, make sure you are hitting the root of the problem when you go to explain the issues with your husband. Making sure you are on target will help you avoid extra conflict and keep you from coming off as a jealous significant other who has trouble sharing her husband's time. Your point in bringing up the issue is not to cut your husband's friends out of his life; it is to make sure they are not monopolizing his time. Making that point clear is vital to having a successful conversation that accomplishes what you need it to. Before you do approach your husband, here are a few things to consider when you've decided it's time for a talk:

- Do you want your husband home because you do not have your own friends to spend quality time with?

- Is it what your husband does with his friends, not how often he does it, that bothers you most?

- Do you not particularly like the friends he has?

By using this list, you will be able to first decide if the issue is a "you" issue or a "him" issue. If you find yourself answering each one "yes," you may have to reconsider your argument. These are all valid feelings for you to have, but accusing your husband of disappearing into friendships based on the above grounds wouldn't be accurate, kind, or addressing the real issue. The real issues in the above cases lie in the fact that you a) do not have your own friends, b) you disapprove of his actions, or c) you are uncomfortable with who he is friends with. None of these problems relate back to your husband prioritizing his friendships over you. If these ring true for you, it is likely your husband is not distracted; instead, you may have your own unmet needs to deal with.

If this is the case, you should still talk with your husband about your feelings. Even if your husband's distraction is not causing the problems, your unmet needs deserve to be addressed and resolved. The key is to detect the real root of the problem and address it there, where it begins, rather than grab at straws and cause more unnecessary conflict.

HELPING HIM KICK THE HABIT

As with any sensitive topic, approach this humbly and with an open mind. Regardless of how right you may be, starting a conversation with hostility and focused anger will only result in a fight, which will prove counterproductive in the end.

Remember to come to the conversation with clear, mature, and useful goals. In order to have a helpful discussion, make sure you are ready and able to do the following:

1. Hear his side of the story so you can better understand the situation.

2. Share your own experiences without being confrontational, angry, critical, petty, or blaming.

3. Reach a resolution that is satisfactory for both parties.

Ideally, your husband will also be ready to follow these three guidelines. It is likely that he will not begin completely receptive to each, but hopefully with your steady insistence, he will see that it matters enough to you for him to take it seriously. Once your husband realizes the importance of solving the issue, he should be ready to approach the conversation as an adult, following the above guidelines.

Of course, being able to follow the guidelines and getting your husband to do so as well is often easier said than done.

Communicating honestly and openly is hard work, but it does get easier. The sooner you and your husband start learning to communicate with each other effectively and respectfully, the better you will get at coming to resolutions when future issues arise.

The communication skills you will develop by successfully bringing your husband back from his distraction will continue to benefit your marriage and other relationships throughout your life. It's hard work, but it's worth it.

WHEN TO SEEK PROFESSIONAL HELP

If you confront your husband and it doesn't seem to be penetrating, then it may be necessary to seek the services of a qualified marriage counselor to assist you both with communicating your thoughts and feelings to one another more appropriately. The issue could be a lack of clarity on your side, an inability to accept fault on your husband's, or simply that you and your husband have problems that go deeper than who your husband is spending his Saturday afternoons with. A counselor will be able to provide an unbiased opinion on which category you and your husband fall into.

When you have exhausted your own patience in communicating your concerns with your husband and are still standing in the same place you started or have actually lost ground, it is clear you are not going to make any headway on your own. Don't torture yourself and add stress to your life by insisting on going at it alone. Make an appointment with someone who can offer professional advice and is trained to deal with these matters.

CLOSING SOLUTION

Although friendship is important for every person, you shouldn't let it interfere with your marital relationship. If your husband is placing his friends ahead of you, it may be hard at first to start the conversation, but communication is key to him understanding how this affects you. Try to approach him when you aren't already upset. Approaching him while you are upset can be counterproductive when bringing a marital problem to light. If you speak from anger instead of love, your husband may come to the conclusion that his friendships are not the issues at hand, your jealousy is. To avoid a misleading conversation fueled by anger, try discussing your frustrations with a close friend or counselor first. This will allow you time to decompress and provide you with another perspective.

Let's take a look back at Steve and Elizabeth:

Elizabeth tried sitting Steve down and discussing how she felt about his relationship with his friends. She let him know that she thought that friendships were important but felt that his friendships were interfering with their marriage. As she was talking, Steve was actually on the phone with a friend listening to a drawn-out story. She didn't realize until she heard a faint yell coming from her husband's direction that while she was talking, he had his hands-free earpiece in and was not paying attention to her at all as she spoke. She had enough! She stormed off into their room without even addressing Steve's disrespect. Elizabeth grabbed a suitcase and packed it. She came out to the living room where Steve was still on the phone, chuckling about whatever his friend had just said. This seemed to be a joke to him.

Steve looked up at his wife and seemed shocked. Elizabeth told him she was leaving for the time being and she didn't plan on coming back until they had spent some time with a marriage counselor and started working their problems out. Steve was speechless. Elizabeth left him on the couch with a stunned expression wondering what had just happened.

It was several months later and numerous sessions with a Christian marriage counselor, but Elizabeth eventually did return home to a different Steve. Through counseling and really working on their marriage, they had found out that they both had some serious issues to work through. Steve began to examine his own avoidant behavior and also why he felt the need to stay guarded with his wife but felt safe with his friends. Elizabeth was also working on making their marriage stronger. She was learning how to be a best friend, not just a wife, and working in communicating clearly with Steve. It was taking a lot of work, but both knew that they had something worth working for, and they weren't going to let miscommunication get in the way.

CHAPTER 8:

MARRIED TO THE CHURCH

PAUL AND AUDREY'S
MINISTRY MISHAP

It was late as Paul pulled into the driveway. Audrey had been waiting for hours for her husband to return home from his speaking engagement at the Holiness Conference across town. Audrey usually tried to go, but she had so many obligations, she wasn't able to attend. Lately, she seemed to have one obligation after the next that kept her from attending her husband's events. At one time, she made her husband's commitments her own. She slowly began to build her own life, though, and started to see that she needed to make time for her own goals and aspirations as well.

Audrey and Paul had been married for fifteen years and had two beautiful daughters in high school. Paul had been in the ministry full time for ten years, but lately all his time was spent in there. As his responsibilities to the ministry increased, the time he had for anything else in life dwindled. He was doing God's work, though, so he figured that his absence at home could be excused.

Paul sighed deeply as he rounded the corner into his cul-de-sac. "Phew," he said out loud as he pulled into his garage and killed the engine. He was tired. It had been a long day, or week really for that matter. Since he had moved up in the ministry, it seemed every week was a long week. That was fine by Paul, though. He felt good about what he was doing and knew that it was benefiting countless people.

Paul felt so blessed to be chosen by God to speak His Word to so many people. It was so much easier to minister in service than communicate with his wife, Audrey, lately. She didn't seem to understand that he needed lots of time to prepare for his messages. He needed study time, prayer time, and he also counseled others. He didn't take his work lightly. It was, after all, God's work. He couldn't understand how Audrey could be selfish when it came to this matter. At the end of the day, she needed to make sacrifices like everyone else. How hard was that to understand?

Paul spent his days counseling individuals in his church and his evenings preparing for messages and speaking engagements. Paul knew his family understood the importance of God's work and the time it demanded away from home, but he did try to at least eat dinner with them nightly. This wasn't always guaranteed, either, but it was his attempt at remaining an active part of their family. Unfortunately, however, more often than not he was pouring over notes or mapping out his schedule for the next week as they dined. There was no time for talk about soccer games, school projects, or even how anyone else's day had gone. He was present, though, so he figured that counted for something.

As Paul turned the key, he stepped into the front entrance and made his way to kitchen to grab something to eat before he went to bed. Paul had gotten caught up after the service with some people who had additional prayer requests that evening and had long missed dinner with his family. As he walked through the living room, he could feel a presence in the room. Paul slowly turned around and saw his wife, still awake and reading beneath the light of a lamp. She was curled up in the oversized chair they had bought as their first piece of furniture together.

"Hello, sweetie," Paul said softly as he leaned down to kiss his wife on the forehead. "I can't believe you're still awake."

"I am," Audrey replied in a chilly tone. "How was service?"

"It was powerful. God really showed up!" Paul explained with excitement behind his words.

"That's really awesome. I thought service would be over at nine thirty tonight? It's midnight." Audrey's words were hard and short.

"Yes, it did end, but you know that people need prayer, and then I stayed and talked to some of the ministers at that church. Why? What's wrong?" Paul said, slightly irritated by his wife's coldness. *Why am I being interrogated?* he thought as he stared down at his wife.

"I just expected you home for dinner and have been waiting all night to hear from you," Audrey said with a sigh. Her face softened, and her expression changed from annoyed to melancholy.

Without responding to his wife's reply, Paul shook his head and headed straight to the bedroom. As he entered the room, he noticed it smelled sweet and was dimly lit with candles. He dropped his briefcase and began pulling off his suit. He turned around and finally noticed that Audrey had on a beautiful lace negligee. Her hair was still done, and she had obviously done her makeup just for the evening. He hadn't even noticed when they were talking.

Paul smiled as Audrey slowly walked over and bent down to blow out the candles. He walked over and put his hands on his wife's waist and leaned in to kiss her and then remembered that he needed to look something up really quickly before bed. He whispered to Audrey that he would be right back and darted from their room to the office.

Audrey lay down to wait. Ten minutes passed then twenty and then an hour. When she realized that her husband had most likely got carried away preparing for whatever event he had next and would not be coming to bed, Audrey drifted off to sleep. Two hours later Paul finally returned to his bedroom to find his wife sound asleep.

UNDERSTANDING YOUR HUSBAND'S PREACHING PASSION

There are many men in the ministry who get so caught up in preaching and ministering to others that they lose sight of their family. This was my own "other woman." As a two-time successive church planter with a young family, I was caught up with ministry and the quest to succeed to the detriment of my family. Fortunately, my beloved wife was wise enough to stir me back to my senses early enough. It was my experience during the time I was resetting my priorities that the idea for this book was born.

Ministry is a hard distraction to argue with for a spouse, and it can be almost impossible to find a balance within it. Although it can be tough, there is a balance and your husband will need to find it if your marriage is going to work. The catch twenty-two to creating a middle ground between dedication to God's work and the family, however, is that the process of finding the balance may be a stressor in and of itself. It is a necessary stressor, though, that will pay off in the long run.

When faced with the difficult task of balancing spreading the Word of God and fulfilling the role of father and husband, your husband may find solace in surrounding himself with the things and needs of the ministry instead of facing the issue head-on. This is an escape that can be easily justified. Some Scriptures are pulled out of context to support this obsolete God-Ministry-Family concept, such as:

> And He was saying to them all, "If anyone wishes to come after Me, he must deny himself, and take up his cross daily and follow Me."
>
> Luke 9:23 (NASB)

> But Jesus said to him, "No one, after putting his hand to the plow and looking back, is fit for the kingdom of God."
>
> Luke 9:62 (NASB)

If anyone comes to Me, and does not hate his own father
and mother and wife and children and brothers and sisters,
yes, and even his own life, he cannot be My disciple.

Luke 14:26 (NASB)

Unfortunately most ministers confuse working for God with
working and walking with Him. The truth is that we cannot
love the Lord less than we love ourselves or anyone else, but
the Bible does not support us loving ministry work more than
ourselves and families. One can die for ministry as many have
done without knowing the Lord. So the Scriptures above talk
about devotion to the Lord but not to ministry work. We are
called to love the Lord deeply with all of our hearts, souls,
and might, but loving God does not translate to the obsessive
ministry visions and self-centered agenda most ministers
invent and impose upon themselves and their subordinates
to the detriment of their marriage and family. Therefore, the
new paradigm I promote is God-Family-Ministry-Works. It
is refreshing to know that many are currently embracing this
concept and even moving their family and ministry forward
more than they had envisaged.

Many times, ministers feel that their sacrifices make them
more spiritual and are proof of devotion, so they reason away their
lack of availability to their wives or family. Whether your husband
is a pastor, elder, or evangelist, he still needs to have a relationship
with you in which there exists a deep level of intimacy. Having
intimacy in a marriage is vital. This level of intimacy doesn't just
promote a healthy marriage; it also teaches us how to have a
deeper connection with God. It was God's purpose for man and
woman to become one. He created Eve as Adam's helpmeet, to
act as a partner, a confidant, a lover, and a guide. God did not
intend for a man to become one with his wife only to put her in
the background once his ministries hit full stride. The day your
husband married you, he made a commitment to you and to God

to devote himself to you. It is important to keep this in mind when questions surface about his role as your husband.

The distraction of the ministry can be a very subtle "other woman" at first because it comes naturally to be zealous in the ministry. Unlike things like hobbies or sports teams, devoting oneself to the ministry is admirable and is unquestionably positive. A man isn't spending time away from home to pursue leisure activities; he is out helping others and spreading the Word of God. The very nature of the issue makes it a difficult one to address for a woman struggling with it.

Remember, though, that a distraction, no matter its source, is typically an avoidance of a deeper issue. This underlying problem may or may not have anything to do with you directly, but it is certainly there if your husband has become absent in your family. He could be feeling inadequate as a Christian, husband, lover, leader, or father and is responding to his own insecurities by burying himself in something he feels will compensate for his perceived shortcomings. Each of these struggles can drive a wedge into the marriage.

To begin restoration on your relationship, you must begin to identify what inadequacy that your husband is dealing with. By pinpointing what it is specifically he feels he needs to hide from, you will be able to better understand him and to help in overcoming his insecurity.

HELPING HIM KICK THE HABIT

If you are able to see where the disconnection is, then you will be able to relate to your husband and walk beside him as he takes on his personal anxieties. You want to be a foundation he can stand on as he addresses the root of his problems being present in your marriage, not an obstacle he must get past. Solving your marriage crisis will be much easier for both you and your husband if you enter into the process with understanding. Every man will have his own personal reasons for placing so much focus and energy into ministry. This is the case because there are a number of motivating factors behind an individual starting a ministry. Your husband may be engrossed in his endeavor because he feels that it is what God needs of him, or he could be thoroughly absorbed in it because his heart is aching for people living in darkness. No matter the cause, though, something has obviously fallen off track if you feel your husband has begun hiding behind his ministry.

Many times, seeking counsel can be a difficult process for a man in ministry. The embarrassment of not having it all together can be overwhelming. Because he is used to being the one with the answers, it may be hard for him to admit that he is struggling within his own life.

A man who counsels himself will also bring a critical eye to a therapy session, so it may take a little longer for him to find the right counselor whom he feels is qualified to handle his marital issues. Be prepared for these hang-ups, and try to be tolerant of his fastidiousness where choosing a professional is concerned.

Being able to help your husband may require a lot of patience and research since you will want a counselor who is not familiar with his ministerial duties. This neutrality can be what seals the deal.

HOMEWORK FOR YOUR MARRIAGE

Although going at it alone may sound hard, it can simply mean doing the legwork first. There are instances where the situation may only be progressing because it has not been acknowledged. By acknowledging the issue, you can stop the miscommunication that may be present between you and your husband.

In order to confront the issue, it will be important that you enter into the discussion without frustration or anger. If you feel that you cannot discuss the issue calmly, go to a trusted friend or talk to a counselor by yourself first to be sure that you are in the mind-set you need to be to ensure that you do not exacerbate the problem. The goal is, after all, to reestablish the unity between you and your husband, not to create a bigger gap between you.

If you decide to take this route, be sure to have a backup plan in place. Many times if approached incorrectly, your husband can either withdraw or lash out. This could push your husband further from you or lead to him simply denying that there is an issue.

WHEN TO SEEK PROFESSIONAL HELP

If you find yourself in a situation in which you have hit an emotional brick wall with your husband, it is advisable to seek professional help, as there may be a deeper issue that is invisible to your eyes. Torturing yourself trying to figure out why your husband isn't receptive to your complaints is not productive or healthy for you or your marriage. Don't allow shame or embarrassment to rule in your decision to seek out professional help. In fact, you should be proud of the fact that you and your husband are so willing to take the steps it takes to ensure your marriage is as good as it can be.

When you do decide that a counselor would be the best option for you and your husband, be sure that you are careful of whom you choose. If your husband's ministry is widely known, then there could be prior knowledge a counselor already has that may disrupt the process. Also, discretion is probably going to be very important to your spouse since he likely wants to maintain a certain image as a counselor himself.

Currently, as a result of many high-profile divorce cases involving popular ministers, many Christians are beginning to look critically into the impacts ministry can have on a minister's marriage when the *God-Family-Ministry* order is altered into *God-Ministry-Family* as many have come to believe and practice. There is no scripture that supports the exaltation of ministry or any vocation above family. Marriage and family are God's heartbeat. It is the beginning of every ministry. A minister who fails to pastor his family effectively should have no business building any outside ministry. However, it takes a transformational experience to get many preachers to embrace the *God-Family-Ministry-Work* paradigm shift.

CLOSING SOLUTION

Remember that when dealing with your husband in his areas of distraction, the process may bring up areas in which you are lacking that you will need to be open to address in order to make real headway. Transparency will be the key in finding the balance for your husband and for eliminating the distraction.

This "other woman" is fed through the inadequacies in the marriage, and as these shortfalls are dealt with, the "other woman" will be dealt with as well. Being able to stop the ministry model woman affair will be a matter of dealing with your issues and helping your husband deal with his.

Let's take another look at what Paul and Audrey are doing now:

Audrey asked Paul to sit and talk to her. She began to share her experiences while growing up in a minister's home. She remembered only spending time with her father when he was at church. She could recall countless school activities that only her mother showed up to. This was a sore memory for her. She hadn't had the opportunity to share any meaningful experiences with her father because he died suddenly before she turned eighteen. She didn't want their children to miss out on what she did.

Paul listened to his wife intently. He realized while she was sharing that she was afraid that she was going to go through this in her adult life as well, that she would have to relive not getting the quality time that she craved from the most important man in her life. Paul was very sympathetic to his wife and could understand her concerns. After he sat and thought for a moment, he began to explain his side of the situation.

Paul shared that knew why he stayed so involved; he wanted his daughters to have a godly father as an example. He remembered growing up in an ungodly home. The only time he went to church was when his mom snuck them all out on Sunday morning while their dad was still sleeping off the night before. He realized as a young child that he did not want his own children to ever feel the way that he did or have to hide their faith in their own home.

After fifteen years of marriage, Audrey heard all this for the first time. She knew that he hadn't been raised in the church, but she had no idea the reason behind it or how it had affected him. She began to understand him more. Audrey was glad that they had sat down and created open lines of communication. She and Paul decided to commit to having these sit downs weekly in order to stay in touch with each. They also agreed to make an effort to spend more time together as a couple and as a family.

CHAPTER 9:

HINDERED BY HARD LIQUOR: DEALING WITH ALCOHOLISM IN A MARRIAGE

ALEX AND SARAH'S LIQUID PREDICAMENT

Alex tiptoed through the living room and down the hallway, making his way to the garage while Sarah was sleeping. He gently turned the knob, trying not to disturb their dog, Rex. Rex barked all the time, at every noise he heard, so he had to be especially quiet. When Alex and Sarah first met in their early twenties, Alex was quite the drinker. It was part of his social life, though, so Sarah rolled her eyes and casually laughed it off when he would fall down in a bar parking lot or spend the day in bed recovering from a wild night. Eventually, Sarah had tamed the party animal, and the two settled down and got married.

Alex and Sarah were now in their forties. They found out early in their marriage that they would not be able to have children, so they began to focus all their time into their careers. Devoting yourself to a career and having a wife that did the same could sometimes lead to life that felt less than complete. Sure, professional success was something to be proud of, but it can't be the focal point of your life. Alex had found something that helped fill those holes, tequila.

Alex had been slipping out and taking sips of his favorite "woman," tequila, for a while now.

As he closed the door, he could still taste the tequila on his lips and tongue. Alex shuffled across the cool cement floor to a giant worn sofa and plopped down, flipping on the TV. They had turned the garage into a kind of lounge area for game nights and poker parties. He put the lip of the bottle to his mouth and tipped it up, opening his throat for the amber liquid to slide down.

Alex loved everything about tequila—the taste, the smell, the warmth he felt as it hit the bottom of his stomach. With each sip, he felt better and better. Alex came out here to relax occasionally, but now it was daily and sometimes all day on the weekends. Alex dozed off with the bottle in his hand.

Sarah pretended to sleep as Alex left the room. She just didn't understand it. What was it that her husband was running away from? Why did he prefer spending the day with a bottle of tequila to spending it with her? Sure, she had put on a couple of extra pounds when she hit her midthirties, but she hadn't drastically changed. Why did he suddenly feel the need to hide away in a bottle? She could tell that he wasn't ever focused on her. His thoughts were always on his mistress, tequila. This "other woman" had clearly taken Sarah's place.

Sarah missed the way things were at the beginning of their marriage before they had both thrown themselves so wholeheartedly into their careers. They would spend hours snuggling in bed. This would happen three or four times a week. Now, though, if they were even sleeping in the same bed, they were faced opposite directions with ear buds in to drown out the noise the other might make.

Alex seemed to be preoccupied with something but would never say what. Sarah had begun to think that his distance was due to the fact she couldn't get pregnant. She had told him the miraculous news that she was pregnant a month ago now, however, and things didn't seem to be changing. Even though Alex said he was happy and excited, Sarah noticed that he seemed to visit tequila even more. As her emotions rose to the surface, Sarah quietly sobbed herself to sleep, hoping Alex would finally come around. *Maybe counseling would help*, she thought as finally fell into a deep sleep.

Alex was awakened by a pounding headache. The best cure for that was another sip. Alex was struggling with Sarah's news of pregnancy. He was going to be a father. He felt excited and terrified. Will he have to give up tequila? And could he even do that? Alex took another swig and laid his head back. His eyes rolled around and finally closed. Alex slept through the rest of the night and half of the next day. It was Saturday. Alex opened his eyes and started patting the couch for his woman, tequila…

UNDERSTANDING YOUR HUSBAND'S INTOXICATING CRUTCH

Battling addictions that come in the disguise of the "other woman" is exceptionally important to deal with. Many times small distractions can become large ones, and if your husband is being distracted by another woman that he calls "alcohol," then it is definitely time to find out what the root of the distraction is.

Alcohol has a way of sneaking in as an extra glass of wine or a little sip of something else stronger and working its way to becoming a full-fledged problem. As Christians, many married couples are hesitant to admit, or expose, this issue. However, if your husband is suffering with alcohol, it is very important that you push past embarrassment and seek out assistance.

Many couples struggle with inadequacies. So don't think that you are the only one. One of the first steps that you can take is to assess how much your husband actually drinks. This can help in identifying how serious this issue is. It could be the beginning of an alcohol problem or an addiction that has grown.

HELPING HIM KICK THE HABIT

It is in your nature as a life partner and a wife to want to help your spouse with any problems that he may be facing. Sometimes in the process of wanting to help, you can become bitter about the problem you are attempting to solve and do more damage than help when addressing the issue, however. In order to avoid this, it is advisable to use someone you trust as a sounding board. This allows you to get your frustrations out before you approach your husband.

The last thing you want to do is to create defensiveness in your husband by blaming or pointing a finger, so the attitude you bring to the discussion is vital. Blame is a fast ticket to a shutdown in any confrontation. Also, using a sounding board may help by ensuring that you are not too upset you may not hear what's important, which is *why* he is running to that "other woman."

In situations involving alcohol and other very serious addictions, it is probably going to be essential that you have a plan to see a professional addiction counselor concerning the issue. There are a lot of facets to addiction that are both mental and physical. It is important to address all of them when searching for a solution, and a professional will be able to do that.

When you have decided to take action, an intervention is necessary for this type of situation, whether it is intervention with a therapist, treatment center, or just the two of you. In most cases, the intervention should include treatment. If your husband does not have a physical addiction and has agreed to participate in counseling, however, the intervention can remain between the two of you.

OVERCOMING SHAME

As Christians, shame likes to step in the way when dealing with more clear-cut problems such as alcohol. Oftentimes, shame can act as an obstacle for couples, preventing them from seeking out the help that they need in their marriage and individually. Don't let shame be the reason that you and your spouse don't seek out help. There are so many different couples who are dealing with exactly what you are facing.

An important part of overcoming shame is helping your husband understand that the problem at hand is greater than him. This allows him to come to grips with the truth that he cannot handle his addiction on his own; if he could, there would not be an argument. Also, reassure your husband that you are not upset with him and that his addiction does not make him a bad person. Always remind him that he is simply someone who is having a difficult time and needs some help dealing with it.

Always bear in mind that your commitment to assisting your husband with this addiction and distraction should not enable him or excuse the behavior but should acknowledge the inadequacies that may have played a role in creating the problem and hence find solution to the problem.

WHEN TO SEEK PROFESSIONAL HELP

Alcoholism is a serious issue that affects millions both directly and indirectly. Proverb 20:1 (NASB) says, "Wine is a mocker, strong drink a brawler, And whoever is intoxicated by it is not wise."

If you feel that your husband's drinking has grown from a coping mechanism to an actual addiction, it is time to seek professional help. There are a number of different routes to take when you've realized that you will need more than communication and desire to fix your marriage. The following are a few options you have in getting help for your loved one who is struggling with addiction:

- Outpatient programs that deal specifically with addiction
- Any program that allow people with like situations support one another and create accountability for one another

- Substance abuse counselors who are trained to deal with the many facets of addiction

- Inpatient programs that are twenty-four-hour facilities designed to remove an individual from his/her environment and use a variety of methods to treat an addiction

- Counseling through the church that will approach the issue from a biblical standpoint.

There is nothing wrong with seeking out assistance from professionals. Although it may seem like reaching out for help is admitting that you are unable to defeat your demons by sheer will and prayer, it is important to remember that we are all flawed. Think of counseling as grace. Grace allows you to admit that you are wrong and without fear of condemnation. Don't go at it alone if you don't have to. It may take some courage and research, but you can find the help that you specifically need. The end results will be well worth it.

CLOSING SOLUTION

Alcohol has affected countless families and caused numerous divorces. Alcoholism has a way of bleeding into every aspect of not only the alcoholic's life but also the lives of his or her family and friends. The disease can cause the fun-loving person you married to become both a stranger and a threat. If this is the case, you should definitely be clear and resolute in demanding that your husband seek help if he wants the marriage to last.

There is nothing wrong with staying in a marriage when a problem has been discovered; however, as long as you don't find yourself enabling your husband and you are both involved in some sort of counseling. Your husband will need a treatment program for recovery, and you will need to be able to talk with someone about how the disease has affected you and your family.

Alcoholism is a serious issue that can be both harmful and fatal and should be treated as such. If you know that your husband is an alcoholic, it is vital that you get help to protect yourself and your family.

Before making a decision, it is best to start individual counseling so that you can make the best choice.

♥   ♥   ♥

Let's look at how Sarah dealt with Alex:

Alex woke up to Sarah standing over him. She was visibly angry.

"Alex, get up and let's talk," Sarah said in a very calculated and rhythmic manner.

Alex rubbed his eyes and stood up. He walked into the living room and sat down. As their dog, Rex, climbed up in his lap, Sarah began to talk.

"Alex, I'm worried about your drinking. It has obviously become a problem, and we need to deal with it. There are so many consequences that this could have, and I love you entirely too much to see you suffer from any of them." Sarah's expression softened as she spoke, and tears began to well in her eyes. She continued to talk about their future and her concerns for his health and the life of their marriage. She discussed therapy and treatment options. Alex listened intently. Somehow he knew this day would come. He wasn't oblivious to what he had become.

Sarah reminded Alex that they were expecting a baby and how every decision they made now would affect that baby. She felt that, while she was still in the beginning trimester, he should seek treatment and they should start both individual and marital counseling. She told him that if he wanted to save this marriage that this would have to happen. By the time Sarah finished, there were tears streaming down her face. She loved Alex so much and wanted this marriage to work.

Alex listened to every word Sarah said, and when she mentioned the pregnancy, he knew he needed to try even harder to make this work. He loved Sarah and definitely didn't want to lose her. Alex promised that he would go to whatever treatment they found for him and that he would deal with this problem. After deciding that he would start treatment immediately, Alex and Sarah held each other and cried together. The next morning Sarah made the phone call.

CHAPTER 10:

DISTRACTED BY DRUGS: DEALING WITH ADDICTION IN THE MARRIAGE

JESSE AND CHRISTY'S NARCOTIC NUISANCE

Jesse was off on another business trip. This would be his third trip for the month. Jesse had just gotten promoted at work and was now on the road nonstop. Even though the time away from his family did bother him, he knew that it was worth the raise and the recognition it would get him from the higher-ups He wanted nothing more than to climb to the top at work, but since he started traveling, his stress levels were skyrocketing. Getting to the top was not going to be easy.

Jesse was an attractive guy with olive skin and piercing green eyes who was always dressed to impress. He was the typical Ivy League frat boy gone professional. He tended to mix partying with his professional activities, just like he had in his Ivy League college days. It started out innocent enough, though. Besides, almost all the people he knew did it too.

Tonight, like many other nights, Jesse was meeting one of his colleagues at an exclusive club. There he would talk business with another man dressed in Armani while young, flirtatious women came by and offered mixed drinks or cigars until Jesse's colleague would offer something a little more exciting than a Glenlevit on the rocks while they talked shop. Jesse knew that the particular partner he was meeting always had a special pick-me-up to help them recover from a hard day. It never failed; inevitably he pulled out a tiny silver container that looked like a cardholder, and Jesse immediately knew what it was: cocaine.

Yes, cocaine was a norm in his travels now. It seemed to be as much a part of his business trips as airplane peanuts and room service. Recently, Jesse had noticed that he craved it when he was home too, but so far he had been able to stave off the desire. He figured it was something like comfort food, a want more than a growing physical need.

The phone rang a little after 8:00 p.m. As usual, it was Jesse's wife, Christy. Christy always called in the evenings to chat and talk about what had been going on at home while Jesse was away on business.

"Hello," answered Jesse.

"Hello, J," Christy said with a smile that you could almost hear. "How was your day today?" she quickly added.

"It was just like all my other days—stressful, long, and draining," Jesse said to his wife somewhat gruffly. It was getting late, and he knew that once he was off the phone a line of cocaine awaited him.

"Oh, I am so sorry, honey. I wish I could be there to help ease the stress for you. We had an okay day here. The kids are all settled after an afternoon of nonstop activities. I have the day off tomorrow. So when do you think you will be home?" Christy rambled on without taking a breath between her thoughts.

"We miss you a lot," she said after a slight pause.

"I am glad to hear everything is going okay there. I miss you all, too. I need to grab something to eat and lay down. Got an early start in the morning. Talk to you tomorrow when I'm back home. Love you!" Jesse said hurriedly, trying to get off the phone.

"Okay, J. I will see you when you get home. Call me if you need a ride from the airport," Christy said as they hung up.

Jesse thought the phone conversation would never end. He quickly changed his clothes and slid into a pair of J. Crew slacks, a Ralph Lauren button down oxford, his favorite sports coat, and met his colleagues in the hotel foyer. Groups of nicely dressed businessmen assembled in the lobby and then hopped into their SUVs and were off to the club.

Within minutes of getting into his friend's Escalade, Jesse was bending over doing his first line of the night. At the club, he maintained his high. As long as you had money and tipped well, a club owner would look the other way, no matter what you were doing. Jesse and his friends took full advantage of this as they sat in a dimly lit booth with bottles of Dom Perignon cluttering the table.

As he reclined a little, laying his head back on the leather seat, he thought about his wife. She would never come into a place like this. The thing was, ordinarily he wouldn't either. Jesse took another line and thought to himself, *How did you get here?* When he was at home, he went to church and Bible study and spent the evenings watching Pixar movies with the kids. When he traveled, however, it seemed that he always forgot to pack his morals. Yes, he was a different man when he left his zip code. Jesse laid his head back and stared blankly at the ceiling. Maybe another line would stop his mind from wandering. Jesse bent over…

As Christy hung up the phone, she realized that Jesse always rushed her off the phone lately. She didn't know how or why exactly, but this new promotion had seemed to drive a wedge in their marriage. Jesse just didn't seem to be the same guy anymore. He seemed distracted and irritable when he was at home. He also didn't seem to act the same toward her.

Christy couldn't help but think that her husband was bored with their marriage or unhappy with their life. She didn't know if it was the monotony of married life or the way things had changed since they had kids, but she was willing to do what she could to save their marriage. She even had begun to work out more in an attempt to regain her husband's attention. She had even lost twenty-five pounds since his promotion. She was now almost back to the size he was when she and Jesse first met in college. She figured that if she kept this up, her husband was bound to notice her and start to love her the way he did when they were first married.

Christy sat down in her now silent house and began thinking about the possibility of seeking a counselor for her and Jesse. They seemed to have a great marriage before this promotion, but she had been noticing that he began slowly changing since his job title had changed. Since he had been spending so much time out of town, he seemed to be a different person every time he returned. The longer he was home, the more agitated he became with Christy and the kids. She knew that something was going on but was afraid to ask what it was.

After sitting in silence and racking her brain as to why her husband had changed so much recently, she finally decided that worrying and assuming weren't getting her anywhere. She went into the bedroom, climbed into her king-size bed, and turned on the TV that was mounted on the wall in front of her. She flipped through some channels and finally settled on an old movie. As actors and actresses in tuxedos and ball gowns danced across the screen, Christy drifted off to sleep.

Jesse finally came to and realized that he was back in his hotel room, but he had no idea how he got there. The ring of the phone was exploding in his eardrums as the front desk called his room for the wake-up call he had made the night before. He had twenty-five minutes to get out the door and to the airport for check-in.

Jesse rolled out of bed fully clothed and grabbed the one suitcase he had brought with him. He proceeded to walk out the door, but just before the door slammed shut behind him, he remembered he had a line in the bathroom. Jesse kicked the door back open and rushed into the bathroom. There on the granite bathroom countertop a rail of white powder sat and patiently waited for his nostril to take it in. He inhaled the grainy substance in one quick breath and hurried off to the airport. He was on his way back home to his family.

As he sat on the plane awaiting takeoff, he glanced at his calendar and noticed that he would only be home three days this time. Jesse breathed a sigh of relief and closed his eyes.

Christy heard the cab pull into the driveway. The kids were excited and ran out to the car immediately. Daddy was home. Christy forced a smile on her face and waited for her husband to enter the house. As Christy waited, she couldn't help but wonder how long he would be in town this time and, better yet, how long would it be before he started blowing up on his family and looked for every reason to leave the house.

UNDERSTANDING ADDICTION AND THE SERIOUSNESS OF CHEMICAL ABUSE

Using drugs as a distraction from life's stressors can lead to a very serious addiction. If your spouse is seeking solace in drugs, you immediately have a critical issue at hand, as drug use is often an indicator of a much bigger problem. Obviously, your husband feels that there is an inadequacy somewhere in his life, and he has taken a destructive path in an attempt to fulfill that insufficiency. There is a wide range of marital inadequacies that can play a major role in your husband seeking the comfort of the "other woman" that we call drugs. However, this particular distraction is a very serious one that is not only damaging to the marriage but can be fatal.

There may have been various signs along the way that were indicative of the approaching problem, but don't be discouraged if you didn't see it coming. Many wives, family members, and friends don't see these signs at all. Oftentimes, it is difficult for an individual to admit that a loved one has a serious problem. Addiction, after all, affects the entire family, not just the addict. It also has a way of placing blame on everyone around. This makes recognizing it tough for many.

Your spouse will need you to be exceptionally understanding but not enabling. There is such a fine line in understanding and "being there" and becoming an enabler. You want to acknowledge that there are valid issues underlying the problem with the "other woman" yet not excuse the ability to make decisions toward change.

If you suspect or are aware that the "other woman" in your spouse's life is drugs, then it may be very critical that you seek out some professional advice on watching certain signs that preclude a more serious addiction. Allowing a third party to assist in intervention will relieve some of the stress and also allow you to be there for your husband in a more supportive role and not the interventionist completely.

BECOMING THE STABILIZING FORCE

In a process where the "other woman" is more detrimental to your husband's health and may have lasting damaging effects on you and the family, it is important to become the stabilizing force through support, intervention, and consistency.

Becoming very solid in your decisions and your level of openness and intimacy will be crucial in showing your spouse that you are still his wife. Your husband will want to see that you are still there for him and that you are not just pointing the finger at him. He needs to know that you are still ready to embrace him, not push him away because of his shortcomings.

Sometimes being more open yourself will assist in your husband feeling comfortable enough to begin disclosing his fears, doubts, or even pain. For men, this may be a little harder, but with some encouragement that they are disclosing in a nonjudgmental zone, it can assist with the disclosure process.

WHEN TO SEEK PROFESSIONAL HELP

Seeking professional help in situations such as a possible drug addiction is highly recommended. Whether it is an addiction or a slight recreational activity, it can be very dangerous. Many times a professional counselor will be able to assist in identifying deeper underlying issues, looking past what lies on the surface. This objective viewpoint on the problem can help you and your spouse to remove the "other woman" from your marriage and aid in bringing back the intimacy and closeness to the marital relationship.

When dealing with addiction, it is easy for both the addict and the spouse to excuse the problem or refuse to accept the severity of the addiction. No one likes admitting that they have lost control of themselves, and no spouse wants to admit that there is that serious of a problem in their family. Fear of stigmatization and long-term consequences of seeking help may seem frightening at first, but it is important to keep in mind that drug addiction can be fatal without the proper help, and nothing could be more tragic than losing your spouse to addiction. New jobs can be gotten and friends and family will grow bored with the news of your problem, but death is permanent. Because of that, nothing should keep you from seeking help when a problem is discovered.

Allowing a third party to assess the marriage in a therapeutic way can be somewhat intimidating but can also save your marriage. It is better to face being uncomfortable than it is to lose your husband to another "woman." Don't let yourself be replaced by addiction; use the therapist to deepen your intimacy and marriage.

When dealing with addiction, timing is everything. Make sure that you have had the discussion about seeking a professional counselor with your husband prior to setting the appointment. It is neither wise nor productive to catch your spouse off guard with this sort of information. The sooner you bring it up, the longer your husband will have to process the information and the more likely he will be to agree to see the counselor. Giving him time to think about everything will make him feel that seeking help was a decision that he made, and it is important for everyone to feel in control of his or her own life. It is important that your spouse feels validated and feels that he is a vital part of the decisions being made concerning your marital health.

Also use judgment. If your spouse is a danger to himself and others around him, then it may be necessary to make a quick decision. Even when forced to make immediate decisions, however, it is important to keep your spouse informed as to what is going on. Keeping the lines of communication open will be critical in closing the door on the "other woman" and opening the door to your marriage again.

CLOSING SOLUTION

Turning to drugs as a crutch can be the result of countless changes in life and is often a means of self-medicating. Many times the distraction of drugs can start from a change in stress levels or performance expectations at work. This could be a new level of stress that your husband may not be used to dealing with, and it can open the door for your husband to unknown territories such as the drugs. Using drugs as a coping mechanism can be a return to a familiar habit or a brand new experience.

If this is new territory then it is important to find the source. However, if your husband has had a previous history with drugs, then it is essential to tackle the area that led to its relapse.

Let's look at Jesse and Christy one last time:

Jesse got out the car and walked in with his kids wrapped around his ankles and knees, clinging to him every step of the way. He caught a quick glance of himself in the mirror that hung in their entryway; he hadn't realized how rough he was looking. This week he had done more "coke" than he ever had on his previous business trips, and it was definitely showing.

Seeing her husband so disheveled, Christy dismissed the kids into the back of the house to play. As Jesse walked over to his wife, he leaned in to kiss her on the cheek. Christy pulled back and stared at Jesse's face, studying it in an attempt to figure out what was going on.

Looking back at his wife, Jesse knew she either suspected something or was upset with him. He walked back to their bedroom and put his briefcase and suitcase down on the bed. Christy followed him into their bedroom.

Christy closed their door and in calm, even tone asked, "Are you drinking or doing drugs?" The question was not yes or no; it was a multiple choice.

"Neither. I'm not doing either of those. Why would you ask me that?" Jesse stumbled over his words.

"You are not yourself, Jesse. You are irritated with me and the kids hours after coming home when you hardly ever see us. Most men would be excited to be home, but you seem angry. You're also constantly leaving when you are here. Not to mention you haven't even noticed that I have dropped four sizes," Christy went through the list of reasons she asked that question.

"It's just this new job, Christy. Look, I'm really stressed out. This is a good thing for us, but it is a lot of work for me. I have a lot on my plate," Jesse responded, his voice getting hard and his eyes narrowing as he spoke.

"Maybe you should talk to your boss about traveling less if it is causing so much stress. It isn't worth the raise if you can't enjoy life anymore," Christy replied.

At that moment, Jesse snapped and started yelling and screaming. He was enraged and became a man who Christy had never met. She had never seen him like this. His words were so loud and venomous that Christy began to tremble. Christy started praying under her breath as he yelled. After Jesse stormed out of the house, she packed overnight bags for her and the kids, loaded up their minivan, and left. Christy drove away from their home and marriage that day hoping never to turn back unless Jesse changed. In the end, the house was sold, and Christy bought a small little townhouse for her and the kids. During the separation, she started counseling and continues to go and is slowly rebuilding her life.

After the sting of the separation, Jesse finally was able to accept that he had a problem and checked himself into a rehab to get the help he needed. Even though they are separated, he still loves Christy and smiles when she drives up to his small apartment to drop off the kids. He hopes that someday she can forgive him and they can rekindle what was once there. If only he would've done this to begin with, he would think, he would have the support of his wife right now and a loving home to walk into instead of an empty apartment with a gold fish.

CHAPTER 11:

THE STRAIN OF CONFUSED SEXUALITY

JEN AND SEAN'S STRUGGLE

J en was doing laundry and noticed the smell of a cologne that her husband, Sean, didn't wear. She wanted to shrug it off and assume it was nothing to worry about, but this wasn't the first time she had smelled odd cologne on her husband's clothes. She inhaled deeply, taking in the full aroma. It wasn't women's perfume, of that she was sure. Was Sean wearing different colognes to meet with other women, or was it another man's cologne? Neither made any sense to her. Jen shuddered at the thought; it made her nauseated and light-headed just thinking about the possibility of her husband having an affair. Jen quickly finished loading the wash and went back down into the kitchen to get ready to cook dinner.

Sean was just finishing up the last of his paperwork at the office. He called in his secretary, Justin, to file away the case he'd just been working on. He watched as Justin walked through his office with a slight swagger. Sean smiled as Justin entered the office and walked over. Justin leaned close to Sean as he spoke.

"Something you need, Sean?" he asked, keeping eye contact with Sean while he spoke.

Slightly flustered by Justin's obvious body language, Sean answered quickly, "Yes. File this when you have the time, please. Thank you."

"Sure. Anything else?" Justin asked, making it a point to touch Sean's hand as he asked.

In a split second, a thousand responses ran through Sean's head. His face became flushed as Justin's skin touched his own. After a short pause, Sean finally answered.

"That'll be all. You can close the door behind you," Sean said as he regained his composure and tried to shove the thoughts he had just entertained from his mind. *This is work, Sean. Not at work*, Sean thought as he packed up his briefcase to head out for the day.

As Sean made his way from his office to the car, he thought about Justin and how he was obviously coming on to him. Justin coming on to him meant that Justin had an idea about Sean's sexuality. He wondered if anyone else had an idea about his secret. Although Justin was his type, he didn't like the idea that he was that obvious and also didn't like that he had to struggle against his impulses at work while being tempted by his secretary. At home and at the office, he was a straight guy with a family, and he had to be sure everyone saw him that way.

Now that work was over, he was ready to get to the one place he knew he could be someone different. He threw his briefcase in his passenger seat, started his car, and headed toward the one place he knew he could be a different Sean.

Sean was on his way to a bar across town. This bar would give him the freedom to be himself, which meant he could actually act on his impulses when he saw an attractive man. Sean had discovered the bar by accident one night but had become a regular and had been sneaking off to go there at least twice a week now.

As Sean made his way to the bar, his cell phone began vibrating in his pocket. Sean pulled out his cell and glanced at the text message he just received from his wife, Jen. Jen wanted to know what time she could expect him home so she could fix dinner. Sean sent a quick text back that he had to work a little late that night but should be able to be home by eight. Jen let him know that shrimp would be waiting on him when he arrived. She knew that was Sean's favorite.

Sean pulled into the parking lot of his new favorite dive and glanced up at the car's clock just before turning the car off. It was only half past five now, and that meant that Sean had two hours before he would have to go home. That would give him plenty of time to meet someone.

Jen saw that Sean wouldn't be home until eight, so she took her time getting ready and then headed out to the grocery store to grab some fresh shrimp for dinner. As Jen went through the laundry basket looking for a pair of jeans, she thought about Sean's text, and, as she did, she became a little suspicious about it. She thought it was strange that Sean was working late because he had said earlier that he didn't have much to with the holidays approaching. He was a lawyer, though, and had crazy hours since they met. Jen pushed the thoughts aside, finished getting ready, and went about her evening.

Jen made her way through the grocery store, pulled back into her driveway at fifteen after seven, and rushed in to get dinner ready. With ten minutes to spare, Jen finally had everything ready. She decided to take the extra time she had to get a little dressed up for the occasion. She slipped into a little black dress, lit some candles, and waited for her husband. Jen had wanted to start trying for a baby. Maybe tonight she could have the baby conversation with Sean over a candlelit dinner and they could start trying.

At fifteen after eight, Sean rushed in, kissed his wife on the forehead, and went straight back to their bedroom. As Sean rushed down the hall, he yelled out over his shoulder that he was going to take a quick shower before dinner. As he whisked by, Jen could faintly smell new cologne. She sunk into her seat, blew out the candles, and waited for Sean at the table.

The reason Jen could smell a strange cologne and Sean was so quick to get into the shower was that Sean had succeeded in meeting someone at the bar. As Sean showered, trying to get the smell of cologne off him, Jen sat at the table alone and wept. She was not oblivious to what was going on; the working late, the cologne, and his distance all made sense now. What could she do, though? How do you even start a conversation like this one?

GRASPING INFIDELITY AND AMBIGUOUS SEXUAL ORIENTATION

Feeling that another woman may be after your husband's attention can be a real stress to you and your marriage. However, when the "other woman" ends up being a man, it can be much more painful and confusing. Not understanding why your husband is attracted to other men is a harsh reality that is sometimes unbearable. Because the betrayal works on so many levels, coming to terms with it can prove to be extremely difficult.

Dealing with this issue can vary in its complexities; the cause of your husband's wandering eye may be the result of something as simple as curiosity and experimentation, but it could also be that your husband has a serious attraction to the same sex. This attraction could either be something that your spouse came into the marriage with, or it could be something that he has recently discovered.

Although the realization that your husband may be interested in the same sex can be confusing and hurtful, it is important that you remain open when you begin the discussion on the topic and that you really hear him when he explains himself. This specific topic is a very multifaceted one, as it deals with both trust being broken in the marriage and also the core identity of your husband.

It is important to keep in mind when you are dealing with this issue that, regardless of what is happening, you are not the root of the problem. Whether your husband has always felt this way or has recently become aware of his feelings for men, you have no control over his same-sex tendencies. Taking responsibility is destructive for you and for the marriage, as feeling that your husband's sexuality is a reflection of you as a person will only create resentment, anger, and a host of other issues that you do not want to carry around with you. It is important to remember this as you are wading your way through the mixed emotions you are bound to have.

While working on your own emotions concerning the problems that your husband's sexuality is causing, it is also important to bear in mind that this is a very confusing time for him as well. If you do feel that this is something you can work past, remember to try to understand your husband to help work him through this instead of being angry and placing blame. What he has done to betray you is not a small thing, but if you want to overcome it, you will have to make the decision to be loving and supportive, even when you may not feel like he deserves it.

When the time has come that you are ready to start working toward rebuilding, the first thing you must do is sit down and have a serious discussion with your husband. Although the conversations will not come easy and can create an immense amount of tensions during their genesis, it is vital that you and your husband create an open dialogue in which to discuss the issue. Many times, misunderstanding born from silence will keep you more reclusive than the actual issue at hand.

Prior to bringing up the issue, it will be very important that you are positive that your husband's "other woman" is truly a man. The last thing you want is to confront your husband about being attracted to other men when he isn't. One's sexuality is very personal, and it also helps define a person. To have one's sexuality questioned, especially by a spouse, is monumental, so never confront in haste.

WHEN TO SEEK PROFESSIONAL HELP

If you find that you are too hurt to discuss the issue with your husband, then it may be important that you find a trusted friend or counselor to speak with on this matter. You may find that after unloading your emotions and thoughts on the subject that you are more capable of listening to your spouse.

However, if you still feel like that will be impossible to discuss without some assistance, then recruit a nonbiased third party to be there while you bring up the issue.

There are so many opinions on homosexuality, but in this situation, it is important that you take the issues to a Christian counselor who specializes in dealing with this type of problem. Homosexuality and other sexual perversions can wreck a marriage faster than anyone can predict. All distractions that create tension and break down the lines of communication in a marriage have the ability to cause a lot of emotional pain and suffering. Dealing with infidelity and sexuality, however, seem to leave a deeper and longer-lasting scar.

> But realize this, that in the last days difficult times will come. For men will be lovers of self, lovers of money, boastful, arrogant, revilers, disobedient to parents, ungrateful, unholy, unloving, irreconcilable, malicious gossips, without self-*control*, brutal, haters of good, treacherous, reckless, conceited, lovers of pleasure rather than lovers of God.
>
> 2 Timothy 3:1-4 (NASB)

Something that must always be considered when dealing with serious marital problems is the children who will be affected. Children add yet another component to the issue of a struggling marriage. If you are hurt, you can imagine how your children will feel. It is best to see a professional therapist before disclosing this type of information to your children. This is only necessary, though, if the behavior is not expected to change and there is a separation that happens.

A great rule of thumb for seeking out professional help is to do so when you feel as if you aren't capable of discussing the issues without placing blame, letting out undue frustration and anger, or just simply can't contain your emotions.

So if you cannot do the following, it means that it is time to look for a licensed therapist for help:

- Discuss the issue without placing blame

- Speaking in frustration and anger instead of openness and love

- Enter the discussion with the intentions of finding a solution, not entering it to berate or condemn him.

- Discuss calmly and rationally the issue at hand without letting emotions guide your words.

If you feel you are unable to do all of these, then you will want a third party to assist you in conveying your thoughts without saying things that are more damaging.

CLOSING SOLUTION

Now that you have just discovered that your spouse is feeling confused about his sexuality and has acted upon his feelings, you may be experiencing a variety of emotions such as fear, anger, shock, sadness, and hurt. It is time to seek out someone to share your emotions with. The key to becoming and remaining mentally and emotionally healthy is to deal with your feelings so that you can begin to speak to your spouse. You may be justified reacting aggressively because you have been betrayed, but it is always good to seek redemptive ways to approach radical issues like homosexuality.

You will need to have a frank conversation with your husband. Whether you decide to involve a trusted and mutual friend, pastor, a counselor, or just the two of you, it needs to be dealt with.

The main purpose of this type of intervention is to:

- Identify if your spouse is actually struggling with homosexuality
- Establish whether or not infidelity has occurred
- Determine if your spouse is wanting to reconcile and deal with the issue
- Make some plans for what's next: counseling, accountability, and anything else you decide as a couple

This conversation is critical to knowing what to do next.

Let's also take a glance at how Sean and Jen handled their situation:

Jen knew she needed to find out if her suspicions were true. She talked with her best friend and decided that she should just schedule a dinner for the pastor to come over. Jen was afraid to confront her husband alone because she didn't know if Sean would be open and honest or if he would be angry.

Pastor Dwaine rang the doorbell. Sean answered the door and greeted the pastor with a handshake and a smile. He was happy to see Pastor Dwaine; he had always thought of him as a good friend and a role model. Sean and Pastor Dwaine talked about last night's game as Sean led the pastor back to the dining room where Jen was setting the food on the table.

Over dinner, the conversation was very casual. After the cleanup, they all sat in the living room for small talk. Pastor began speaking about the importance of communication in a marriage. While discussing this, he started asking how the two of them were. This opened the door for Jen to say something.

Jen leaned forward and began to talk, but suddenly she felt like she had swallowed a rock. She began to explain her feelings and concerns but felt uneasy speaking so candidly to Sean. The pastor picked up that she was holding back and edged her forward. With the pastor's support, she proceeded, explaining how she was constantly smelling men's cologne on Sean's clothes that was definitely not his and how his late nights didn't always add up.

The pastor shifted the topic to give Sean the floor. Sean's palms were damp and clammy, and he could feel the heat rising off his body as he sat in the hot seat.

"I know that I need help for this," he said, staring down at his trembling hands as he spoke. "I have been…I have been having an affair…having affairs…with men for a few months now."

Shocked and horrified at what her husband had just said, Jen got up and left the room. She thought that she was ready to hear him admit it, but once the words were out there, it was real and she couldn't' handle it at all. She needed a minute to compose herself. She sat on the bed in the guestroom and just took deep breaths while she waited for Sean's words to sink in.

Sean continued speaking after Jen had left the room and was still talking when she returned. Sean said there were some issues that he was a little embarrassed to speak about in front of his wife. The pastor asked the couple if they were interested in starting formal marital counseling. Sean and Jen immediately agreed that they were. They made their first appointment with the pastor, and then he said they would continue this conversation later when they both had time to think about it.

After the pastor left, Jen moved her stuff into the spare room. She needed to work through the pain of betrayal and confusion before sharing a bed again. Sean understood, and they spent the night reorganizing and slept in separate rooms. They would have a real session tomorrow. Neither knew what the future held, but they both knew they loved one another and they were willing to try. As Sean lay alone in bed that first night, he thought about everything that he had done and began to feel remorseful for everything. He had been curious, yes, and he had let his curiosity take control over him, but that was not who he was or wanted to be.

CHAPTER 12:

A PORNOGRAPHY PREDICAMENT

BRAD'S ADULT VIDEO VICE

B rad was leaned over his laptop with his headphones on. The light from the screen flashed on his face as he sat engrossed in the images that were before him. There were all kinds of women with all kinds of "specialties," and they were only a click away. He took full advantage of that convenience as he sat alone in his office, his eyes glued to his computer screen.

Brad was in his man cave, the place where he could do whatever he wanted. Stretched out across his comfy couch, Brad watched video after video for at least two hours without interruption. As he saw his wife's shadow approach, he quickly closed the window and was now watching a seminar on sales. His wife, Krystal, leaned over and whispered in his ear, "When are you coming to bed?"

Brad looked up, kissed his wife, and mumbled back a response. As Krystal left the room, walking slowly in almost a waddle with her hands supporting her back and her protruding stomach preceding her, Brad began shutting down his computer.

Brad watched his wife, who was seven months pregnant, waddle across the room. She looked so different than she did when they got married. Her once constantly bronze skin was now pale since she had to quit tanning. Her petite, athletic frame had been replaced by a much different one, with a round belly, swollen ankles, and every part of her retaining so much fluid that she looked puffy all the time. Yes, she was quite a different person now.

Brad was excited about having a baby and loved that his wife was too, but he didn't realize how much her body would change in the process. It wasn't that he didn't love her, but it was strange to have someone physically change so quickly. It didn't always feel like the Krystal he married now that she was so different. She looked different, acted different, and even felt different. It was a lot to take in.

Brad made his way from the man cave to the bedroom and lay down beside his now pale and swollen wife. He lay there awhile with his arms around his wife. As she drifted off lying in his arms, Brad gently moved her over. He would watch a little bit more, just until he got drowsy, and then go to sleep.

He grabbed his iPhone from the bedside and began to watch a video he had e-mailed himself that night. He wasn't very interested in his wife at that time, so this would keep him from going insane during the pregnancy.

Krystal had been awake the entire time that Brad was watching the video. She slightly opened one eye when she realized he was watching something and immediately knew what it was. She felt disgusted and hurt but didn't know how to deal with the situation right then, so she closed her eyes and tried to go to sleep.

OVERPOWERING PORNOGRAPHY

If pornography is causing a strain in your marriage, you are certainly not alone. There have been many marriages that have suffered from a spouse's use of pornography. Your husband is struggling with an area that many men and husbands are. Understanding exactly what the lack is that is driving him to this "other woman" is vital in overcoming the pornography problem.

As the wife of a man who has an unhealthy obsession with pornography, you may assume that an inadequacy in your sex life is the cause of your husband's newfound fascination. However, many times this is not the case. In many instances, the issue could be more a problem in the relationship or with intimacy. Being able to connect with your lifelong partner is essential to the overall health of the marriage. If that connection is damaged or broken, there can be serious consequences for the marriage. If you are finding that your husband's "other woman" is pornography, then you should begin asking questions and being observant in order to discover what is lacking in the relationship that is causing him to stray.

The main thing to remember when you first suspect a problem with pornography is to observe first and watch for odd behaviors that indicate that he is spending time, and too much of it, watching pornography. Many times, obtaining this information can be as simple as asking your husband what he is watching and waiting for the response or checking the Internet history periodically to see what web pages show up.

If the pornography is a serious problem, your spouse may become defensive and the conversation could take a turn for the worse. To avoid this, always approach the subject in an unassuming way, making inquiries, not accusations. Handling the problem in this way and gauging your husband's reaction allows you differentiate a serious problem from a topic that may be open for discussion.

WHEN TO SEEK PROFESSIONAL HELP

If you are uncomfortable with confronting the issue alone, then it would be advisable to find a neutral third party to discuss the issue with. This would preferably be a counselor.

Seeking professional help is always a step that many have trouble with in terms of timing. There may not be a magical timeframe that you have in mind when the discussion begins; however, you should think about looking for a marriage counselor when you are unable to communicate your thoughts, feelings with your husband, or you feel that he may have some extreme reactions to being confronted.

It can be hard to seek professional help because you and your husband may feel some shame with exposing the "other woman." Do not let this stop you from seeking help, though; pornography is something that can be dealt with, and it most certainly won't be new to the counselor.

It is not shameful to seek out help. Reaching out for help is not a sign of weakness; it is a testament of your commitment to your marriage. You should feel proud of yourself for being so willing to do what it takes to save your marriage.

CLOSING SOLUTION

Pornography has become a major factor in many marital conflicts and even divorce. Looking at current statistics and talking to divorce lawyers offer proof of its detrimental effects on marital bliss. Within the last few years, a substantial number of marriages have come to an end because of problems caused by pornography. As the Internet has expanded and access to this temptation has grown drastically for men and women, the issue has only become more alarming. Pornography feels inescapable at times, as we see hints of it nonstop any time we browse the Internet. For so long, Christians thought that their husbands and wives were exempt from this temptation. This could not be farther from the truth, however. Many Christian men who have never struggled with pornography are being lured into the seduction of adult videos. It can begin accidentally or with the intention of "just this one time." It doesn't take long, though, for the one time to escalate into a habit. Becoming free from pornography requires some work. You may have to help your husband read and meditate on this Scripture:

> So put to death anything that belongs to your earthly nature. Get rid of your sexual sins and unclean acts. Don't

let your feelings get out of control. Remove from your life all evil longings. Stop always wanting more and more. You might as well be worshiping statues of gods.

Colossians 3:5 (NIV)

The problem with pornography is that once you have opened the door, it can be very hard to close.

If your husband is battling pornography at an addictive level, you may need to seek some help. Addiction to pornography, which can also be sexual addiction, is like any other type of addiction; it is very hard to stop. You will need to have understanding, patience, and a willingness to forgive as your husband deals with this addiction.

Take another look at Brad and Krystal:

Brad and Krystal decided to talk with a counselor. Krystal talked to Brad about her concern for their marriage and explained that it was important to her that they see a counselor. Brad agreed, and so there they were now waiting in the lobby for their first appointment to begin.

As the counselor called their last name, Krystal stood up with Brad beside her. As they went back to the counselor's office, she used him as a support to walk. When they were in session, Krystal used the example of her leaning on him to walk as a metaphor for their marriage. She told Brad that she depended on him to be a support and stabilizer. Krystal's statement helped begin the conversation about the problems in their marriage, and they were on their way to change.

CHAPTER 13:

THE MOST DEADLY GAME: ONLINE OBSESSIONS

KEVIN AND AMY'S INTERNET DISCONNECTION

Kevin rushed in the front door from work. He threw his jacket on the couch and kicked off his shoes. He couldn't wait to start gaming for the evening with his Internet buddies. Kevin was young but didn't seem to act too much older than a high school kid sometimes. His immaturity could actually be charming in some instances, providing him with an air of innocence, but it could also be a little exasperating for his wife.

Kevin and Amy had not been married very long; it would actually be two years that week. Kevin met Amy in college, and they dated their entire college career until he proposed to her the night after graduation. Now they were married and in the real world, but Kevin seemed to be clinging to some parts of his juvenility: online video games.

Kevin made his way to the computer room. He plopped down in his leather office chair, logged in, and settled in for some serious game playing. His night was officially spoken for.

Amy got home late that evening. As she walked through the front door, she could already hear Kevin playing the game in the study, which had been turned into his gamer's cave. She yelled hello and waited a second for a response. He was way too engrossed to notice or hear her. She walked into the kitchen and grabbed a personal pizza from the freezer. She already knew having dinner with her husband was out of the question.

After finishing her pizza, Amy warmed up leftovers from the last time she had tried to make dinner for the two of them. She heated up some fried chicken, macaroni and cheese, and green beans for Kevin and took it into the computer room. She put the plate of leftovers beside him. Without even looking up at Amy, he mumbled a quick thank you and began stuffing his face. He finished eating but stayed fixed on the game.

Amy had picked up the house, showered, and was in bed watching TV, and Kevin was still hidden away in his gamer's cave. While Kevin stared at a computer screen and shot enemy soldiers, Amy had drifted off watching the *Late Show*. When she woke up, she looked to her left to see an empty spot beside her and then to her right to see that it was past midnight.

Kevin was still immersed in his game. He couldn't walk away because he wasn't just winning; he was breaking a personal record! In the midst of his excitement, Kevin finally glanced over to see how late it had gotten. It was now close to one. High score or no, he did have to get up pretty early. He decided it was probably best to call it a night. He would pick up where he left off tomorrow. He needed to recharge his batteries to continue his record-breaking game anyway, so he logged off the computer and made his way down the hall to the bedroom where his wife had been for hours.

Kevin threw himself down and the bed and was out within minutes. Amy woke up the next morning, and Kevin was already gone. She climbed out of bed and began getting ready for work. As she poured her fist cup of coffee, she wondered if Kevin would disappear in his cave yet again tonight. Today was their anniversary, but she knew that it would probably slip his mind since their wedding day didn't have to do with online gaming. As she thought about how true that really was, she took a deep breath in, and her heart ached a little. Had the computer replaced her? Would she ever be the reason he rushed home again?

As Amy got into her car, she realized that another woman was not the only thing that could steal your husband from you.

GETTING TO THE ROOT OF AN INTERNET INTERRUPTION IN YOUR MARRIAGE

Although the distraction of technology is a new issue, it definitely has become an "other woman" in many a marriage. Many times the fascination with the Internet and computers is normal and healthy, and even helpful, in a constantly advancing technological society. There is limitless information and countless positives to taking advantage of the Internet. Because of this, it can be hard to distinguish between a healthy curiosity or an advantageous interest and a harmful fixation.

An unhealthy distraction that may pose as a threat to the marriage is signaled by the importance that your husband has given the Internet. When it seems that his focal point has become his computer screen and everything else is falling by the wayside, it is time to start reevaluating his priorities. Here are some questions to ask when considering whether or not your husband's Internet fascination is a healthy one:

- How much time is being spent on the computer?
- Can your spouse be interrupted?
- Does your husband spend more time on computer than with you or the rest of the family?
- Do you find that family or couple time is interrupted with his Internet games, no matter where you are (due to access through mobile devices)?

These are a few questions to use in analyzing your husband's dedication to the "other woman" and the consequences it is having on your marriage. His Internet affair may be in the early stages, and in this case a simple conversation bringing awareness can solve the issue. However, if it is more in-depth than that, then you may have to deal with any frustration and blame issues you have first. After you are able to talk through the issue with a close friend, then you will be able to confront your husband with the issue.

Remember that when you are confronting that you should be doing more listening than talking. The purpose of bringing up the problem is not to push blame or to start a fight, so take the time to understand why your spouse has allowed this distraction to turn into another woman. There may be some inadequacy in the marriage or intimacy issues that have driven your husband to turn to Internet gaming. Be willing to listen and provide support when you start discussing the root of your husband's problem.

HELPING HIM KICK THE HABIT

If you want to be able to assist your spouse with this distraction, you will have to be understanding and open throughout the process. You will want to find out about the specifics about the distraction that you are facing; whether it is a game or a social networking sites like Facebook, Twitter, or Myspace, what it is that draws him to the distraction, and why he feels the distraction deserves so much of his time. Knowing the details will help you with understanding what void that the game fills for him. Even though you may not completely grasp his fascination, it opens your mind to alternatives and reasons why the "other woman" has precedence in his life.

Coming into the conversation with an open mind and loving heart can do more than just break the ice and create a space to discuss the problem at hand. Sometimes showing some interest in what your husband is doing can open his eyes to realize that he really does enjoy spending time with you. This may also give you a chance to ask questions about the game and what he likes about it. These questions will also help you regain your husband's attention, directing the focus back to you and your family instead of the game.

WHEN TO SEEK PROFESSIONAL HELP

There are some times when online games or the Internet fill a void that is not related to your marriage. If your husband's issues are deeper, seeking out a counselor will prove beneficial for both the marriage and your husband as an individual.

Finding an appropriate therapist is time consuming and can become overwhelming. However, if you are able to briefly discuss some of the reasons that this online "other woman" is around, then you will be able to find a Christian marriage therapist who deals with this issue specifically.

No matter what therapist whom you begin to see, it is important that you inform your spouse the intention for counseling and why you think it may be helpful. Explain that the sessions are not just for him but for you too. Reiterating that the problem is both of yours will help avoid putting your husband on the defense. Also remember when discussing the issue with the therapist not to push the blame completely on your spouse, as you may play a bigger role in the problem than you realize.

Be open and be honest in your sessions. Let down your guard, and let your husband and therapist in to understand your viewpoint. Always be open to hear your husband and his concerns and complaints as well. You should enter into therapy as a team working at the same goal, not as opposing teams trying to defeat the other. To bear one another's burden is a powerful reciprocal truth.

CLOSING SOLUTION

In a fast-paced world, the technological devices for convenience are increasing daily. It is hard to compete with something that is ever changing and always getting better. Your husband will need to deal with his gaming and/or social networking like an addiction. He will need to wean himself and learn moderation.

It isn't uncommon to see men become obsessed with online distractions. As a wife, you need to help him find that balance.

Let's see how Amy and Kevin began dealing with Kevin's addiction to virtual reality games:

After returning from a dinner date for their anniversary, Kevin went straight back to his gamer's cave to start up where he left off the night before. Sitting in the living room all alone, Amy was becoming quite frustrated with Kevin. She decided it was time to confront him with this. She decided that she would talk to him the next evening, since she realized at that moment she was too angry and hurt to have a productive and civil conversation.

The next day, Kevin came home early, and Amy was waiting for him. He was pleasantly surprised by his wife being home already; she was always getting in late from work. Right as Kevin walked in, Amy asked him if they could talk before he started the computer up. Kevin seemed a little caught off guard by Amy's straightforwardness and persistence, so he stood for a minute without responding. Amy went on to explain that it was important to their marriage to talk tonight.

Kevin slowly walked to the couch to sit beside his wife. As he sat down, Amy began to talk.

"I want you to know, first of all, that I have no problems with you playing games online. I know it is something that you have a lot of fun doing, and I am okay with that," Amy explained.

"Okay," Kevin replied, waiting for the catch.

"You've just been so immersed in them lately. I feel like I live alone sometimes." Amy finished her sentence then waited for Kevin's response.

"I know. I know," Kevin said, reaching out for his wife's hand. "I have gotten really caught up the last couple of months. It's silly. I know. I just get carried away."

"I think that we need to find a compromise. Something that allows you to play your game but also gives our relationship the time it deserves," Amy said as she held her husband's hand.

Amy and Kevin decided that a schedule that set aside days that they would spend together and days that he could spend online gaming would work for them best. After they agreed on a schedule (five days were Amy's and two days were Kevin's to spend on the computer), they went out for a romantic evening together.

CHAPTER 14:

THE TELEVISION
TEMPTRESS

ROB AND STEPHANIE'S TV TROUBLE

"Happy anniversary, Stephanie!" Rob exclaimed as his wife walked into the room.

"Wow, that's great, Rob," Stephanie said in a less-than-enthusiastic voice, looking at the "surprise" Rob was alluding to that was now the focal point of their bedroom.

Rob was so pleased with himself. He had finally done it; he had gotten a flat screen for the bedroom. They could now enjoy television from the comfort of their own bed and snuggle without Rob worrying about Stephanie getting up and going to bed. Rob had replaced the cozy fireplace in their bedroom with a built-in entertainment center and the best flat screen he could find. He had really done it now.

Rob was totally in love with Stephanie and had been for more than thirty years. Their kids were all grown and moved out, and it was like he and Stephanie were getting to know each other all over again, which was a good thing because he truly loved her, but he also loved watching his TV shows.

Rob was an older gentleman with salt-and-pepper hair and had a rough look to him. He had worked construction all his life, and, even when not on a work site, he looked the part of a construction worker because of industry stains on his skin.

Rob had lived life doing hard labor, so he had developed quite an affinity for television, as it had for decades offered him relaxation after long days with the jackhammer. Television had become his nightly mini-vacation, a reward for spending hours on end swinging a sledgehammer.

Rob knew that he spent too much time in front of the TV, but it had been his guilty pleasure for years, so he couldn't really see the use in changing anything at that point. It was comfortable to him. Listening to sitcom couples bicker over silly misunderstandings and Dave's top ten had become a part of his routine, and he didn't see why he should change his routine. Rob, like so many of us, was a creature of habit.

At around seven, Rob jumped into bed and started watching the evening news while Stephanie made something to eat in the kitchen. Stephanie sat at the dining room table eating a chicken salad sandwich and waited for Rob to come down to join her. She waited and waited…and waited. Finally, she settled into the recliner and started to read. After an hour or so of agitated reading, she finally went to see what her husband was doing. As she walked into the bedroom, she saw why he hadn't made it downstairs. Rob had dozed off watching TV.

Stephanie walked back out of the room and down the stairs to the kitchen. She could not believe this. She and Rob finally had time to just enjoy one another, and he would still rather watch TV than do something with her. He was so dedicated to his precious primetime schedule that he bought a TV for their thirtieth anniversary! Stephanie thought they may go on a second honeymoon or Rob might get her a day at the spa, but what she came home to was a monstrosity that was only going to eat up more of her husband's time. *Happy anniversary to me*, Stephanie thought as she was slumped over the table with her elbows propped on the wood surface and chin resting on her balled fists.

Stephanie had been through so many changes in thirty years. She had gone from slender to plump and back to a medium build. She was an exceptionally beautiful Puerto Rican woman who was raised in Bronx, New York, and moved to Seattle for college where she met Rob, then married and had his five children. She was fifty now, though, without kids to raise and feeling great. She was ready to finally live her life to the fullest.

Stephanie turned on the Christian radio station and started cleaning up the kitchen. She had decided that she would tidy up a bit since Rob was already snoozing upstairs while *Everybody Loves Raymond* played in the background of his light snoring. She finished wiping the countertops then poured a glass of wine and grabbed her book again. Stephanie sipped her wine while she read *A Tale of Two Cities*. When she got sleepy, she returned to the bedroom to her sleeping husband. She turned the TV off and climbed into bed.

As Stephanie woke up the next morning, the TV was already on and Rob was getting dressed while he stared into it. She yawned and walked slowly to the kitchen to put on a pot of coffee. Now that TV had invaded their room, she couldn't help but feel sad. Rob had moved his other love in the bedroom, and Stephanie knew she couldn't compete. Rob rushed past her as he kissed her quickly and then ran out the front door. As he pulled out the driveway, she sat down to have breakfast alone.

UNDERSTANDING THE BOOB TUBE OBSESSION

Entertainment can be very addictive. Television shows are created to draw you in and keep you coming back week after week. It takes a lot of self-control to resist the pull to watch television all the time. There are endless reasons that we immerse ourselves in fictional sitcoms and late-night comedy shows. There is nothing wrong with having a favorite program, either. When *every* program becomes a favorite program, though, and you begin to spend more time with the Cosbys than your real family, there may be a problem.

Your husband may be watching television because he is trying to escape, but many times if you simply bring up alternatives when you confront him with the problem, the suggestions alone can help steer your husband in the right direction. He is likely not consciously choosing television over you and your family; he may just need a nudge to wake him up.

Television may merely be filling an empty space for your husband, which is the case for many people. When there is nothing else to do around the house, it is easy to flip on the TV. We all spend most of our time dealing with the stress of work; television is a welcome break from that. If your husband's TV routine has started to take away from your relationship, though, it is time to sit down and have a talk about what is going on. The first thing to approaching this "other woman" is to find out what she is doing for your spouse.

- Is she simply giving him something to do?

- Does she merely entertain?

- Is she an escape from intimacy?

- Was she originally just a filler of time but has become addictive?

Identifying what the television is doing for your husband will help you to better understand what you are up against. You may just need to bring the issue to his attention or deal with the problem by offering alternatives.

HELPING HIM KICK THE HABIT

Offering new ways to spend quality time together is a great way to help your husband do something other than spend his spare time in front of the TV. You can help him by making yourself available to do other things. Try to engage in things that you both will enjoy, or even dust off an old hobby you both had before life was filled with your children's activities and obligations. If you want to lure him from focusing on the TV, you can begin to lure him by joining him but doing things such as:

- Ask to pick a movie to watch
- Change the room environment to more romantic for the television show
- Cook dinner and make it special

If your spouse doesn't respond well to these ideas, then he may need to be confronted in a more straightforward manner. Remember when you begin the discussion, though, not to point fingers. Open up by trying to understand what he is getting from this issue. Coming into the discussion in this way will prove to be advantageous for both of you.

WHEN TO SEEK PROFESSIONAL HELP

When the problem has been confronted and your spouse is nonresponsive, it is time to seek the assistance from a counselor. His nonresponsive action is a way of letting you know his problem is deeper than a simple distraction or time filler. He may feel there is a lack of intimacy in the marriage, be using the distraction to avoid communication, or suffer from other feelings of inadequacy.

Counseling can be very helpful in identifying underlying areas that need to be dealt with. Even though this may initially be for your husband, there may be some issues and areas that you want to deal with as well. Many times throughout your marriage you may think and talk about your spouse's shortcomings; however, this could be an opportunity to handle your own perceived faults as well.

Marital counselors are most appropriate for dealing with this type of concern, as they specialize in handling couples and the issues that arise in their relationships. The marital counselor can and usually will see you individually, as well as together, to work on issues that require some one-on-one time.

There are many Christian counselors who may be of help in dealing with the issues at hand in terms of the beliefs and standards that you are looking for as a Christian. A marital counselor is a professional and can also honor certain belief and values systems if they are communicated with them in the beginning.

CLOSING SOLUTION

Sometimes TV is simply a way of entertainment when bored or alone. This distraction is so easy for people to get caught up in. If your spouse is struggling with TV and it moves in front of you on his list of priorities, then it may be very beneficial and helpful to bring this issue out into the open and let him know how you feel.

As his wife, you will need to remain understanding when you voice your complaints and communicate clearly with your husband that you want more time with him. Explain your feelings and thoughts in a nonjudgmental and nonabrasive way so you can come to a compromise instead of a standoff.

Let's see where Rob and Stephanie found their compromise:

Stephanie knew something would have to be done about Rob's constant TV watching. She was quite sure that this would be detrimental to their marriage in its latter years if they didn't nip it in the outlet. Stephanie wanted to have quality time with her husband instead of sitting in a silent living room while he watched *Seinfeld* reruns upstairs. They had sent their kids off into the world, and now they finally had plenty of time to spend together.

Stephanie came into the room, and Rob was watching TV. She moved in between her husband and his beloved flat screen.

"Think we can talk, honey?" Stephanie asked with softness in her voice.

"Sure thing, Steph," Rob said as he threw his legs over the side of their bed and sat up to look at his wife. "What's up, pumpkin?

Stephanie turned off the TV and sat down next to her husband. She looked at him and began to talk.

"I just feel like I never see you anymore," she explained, "and we should be able to really enjoy each other now. You are glued to this television, though, and I am beginning to really hate that flat screen time thief mounted on the wall. I think I may be jealous of it, Rob."

"Well, why wouldn't you be? That's forty-eight inches of high definition," Rob said jokingly, pulling Stephanie to his side. His expression suddenly changed from jovial to serious.

"No, hon, it isn't that I don't want to spend time with you. I just don't feel like I know you very well. We have spent decades raising kids, and I'm afraid that maybe we're different now, and I don't want to find out if that's true."

"Sure we're different, Rob, but we're different in a good way. We get to start again now and fall in love again with just the two of us. I knew when I married you that we would change, but that doesn't mean in a bad way," Stephanie said as she was rubbing her husband's back. "I can't wait to get to know you gain."

Rob looked back at his wife and smiled. She may have changed in some ways, but she was still definitely the person he fell in love with. Rob and Stephanie decided that to begin to understand each other more, they would start having date nights. During these date nights, they would get to know each other all over again.

FINAL THOUGHTS

It takes perseverance, dedication, and commitment to make marriage work. From reading this book, you would have noticed that much emphasis was placed on the wife. You would have also realized that the focus is on redeeming the marriage relationship rather than bailing out. Much consideration was given to some practical steps that may be required to resolving a particular issue. I have also consistently recommended the ministry of qualified Christian counselors or experienced ministers when frank discussions with your husband fail. All of the above emphases are deliberate. The sequel, *The Other Man*, will hopefully make up for whatever lapses or questions that may be on your mind about what you have just read.

One thing worth mentioning here is the power of prayer. Couples who spend time praying together at least once a day will eliminate most of the issues discussed in this book. Nothing refreshes and replenishes marriage like spending quality time together, and praying together helps to reinforce all the virtues that enhance intimacy in marriage. You will do your marriage a lot of good when you pray with your spouse regularly.

We have more marriage-enriching resources available for you in our website: http://familylifecentre.net.

You can also contact our ministry for speaking engagements through the website.

Because of popular demand, we have created a website that offers free pre-counseling services on a wide range issues but specifically on relationships at http://www.transformation-centre.com.

Our team of registered Christian counselors will be glad to help you in any way we can. Through the website, we offer both online and telephone counseling services. This is easily arranged by filling the contact form on the website, and we will connect with you within twenty-four hours.

Here are other ways to connect with us:

Facebook:
@transformationcentre
@transformation family life centre

Twitter:
@godwinude
Blog: http://godwinude.com

If this book has helped you in any way, kindly pay it forward to someone you care about. There is a huge demand for marriage-enriching materials worldwide. The modern and post-modern ideologies are destroying the marriage institution globally, especially in America. Consider every married couple you know as a beneficiary of the information in this book. Help us extend our ministry by blessing them with copies of this book. Those who help marriages are peacemakers. "Blessed are the peacemakers, for they shall be called sons of God" (Matthew 5:9, NASB).

Thank you for being a part of the solution!

Shalom!

Godwin & Blessing
Transformation Family Life Centre (TFLC)
Surrey, BC